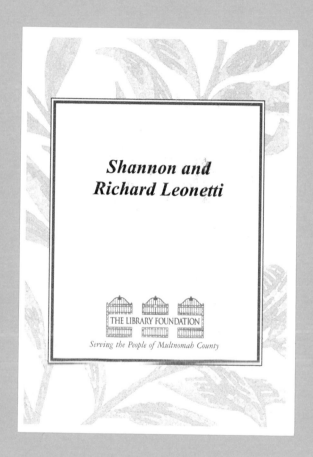

BEAUTIFUL INTERIORS

An Expert's Guide to Creating a More Livable Home

BEAUTIFUL
INTERIORS

An Expert's Guide to
Creating a More Livable Home

Text by Charles D. Gandy, FASID
Photographs by Chris Little
Foreword by BJ Peterson, FASID

Sterling Publishing Co., Inc., New York
A Sterling/Chapelle Book

Chapelle, Ltd.:

Jo Packham

Sara Toliver

Cindy Stoeckl

Matthew DeMaio

Editor: Matthew DeMaio

Art Director: Matthew DeMaio

Copy Editor: Christine Allen-Yazzie

Staff: Areta Bingham, Donna Chambers,
Susan Jorgensen, Barbara Milburn,
Lecia Monsen, Kim Taylor, Desirée Wybrow

If you have any questions or comments, please contact:

Chapelle, Ltd., Inc.,
P.O. Box 9252, Ogden, UT 84409
(801) 621-2777 • (801) 621-2788 Fax
e-mail: chapelle@chapelleltd.com
Web sites: www.chapelleltd.com

Library of Congress Cataloging-in-Publication Data

Gandy, Charles D.
Beautiful interiors : an expert's guide to creating a more livable
home / text by Charles D. Gandy ; photographs by Chris Little ;
foreword by BJ Peterson.
    p. cm.
"A Sterling/Chapelle Book."
Includes index.
ISBN 1-4027-1607-9
1. Interior decoration--Handbooks, manuals, etc. I. Little,
Christopher. II. Title.

NK2115.G247 2005
747--dc22
                                                                2004018555

10 9 8 7 6 5 4 3 2 1

Published by Sterling Publishing Co., Inc.
387 Park Avenue South, New York, NY 10016

Distributed in Canada by Sterling Publishing
c/o Manda Group, 165 Dufferin Street
Toronto, Ontario, Canada M6K 3H6

Distributed in Great Britain by:
Chrysalis Books Group PLC
The Chrysalis Building
Bramley Road
London W10 6SP, England

Distributed in Australia by:
Capricorn Link (Australia) Pty. Ltd.
P.O. Box 704
Windsor, NSW 2756, Australia

Printed and Bound in China.

Sterling ISBN 1-4027-1607-9

CONTENTS

Foreword	**8**
Introduction	**10**

Understanding the		**Setting the Stage**	**42**
Fundamentals	**12**	Floors	45
Line	16	Walls	48
Rhythm	20	Ceilings	50
Scale	23	Doors	52
Shape	26	Windows	55
Form	26	Lighting	56
Balance	28	Color	60
Mass	32		
Texture	34		
Pattern	35		
Closure	36		
Variety	40		
Proportion	40		

Embellishments	**64**	**Specific Spaces**	**86**	**The WOW Factor**	**122**
Furniture	70	Entry Halls	88	Simplify, then Exaggerate	125
Fabric	76	Living Rooms	90	Eclecticism	126
Window Treatments	80	Dining Rooms	92	Accessorizing	129
		Kitchens	98	A Final Word	138
		Bedrooms	101	Designers	140
		Guestrooms	108	Acknowledgments	142
		Bathrooms	110	Index	143
		Powder Rooms	114		
		Home Offices	116		
		Home Libraries	118		

FOREWORD

Charles Gandy, a masterful storyteller and designer, has collaborated with his favorite photographer, Chris Little, to create this informative work outlining the ABCs of interior design.

Charles and Chris have worked as a team for two decades: Charles, as the founder of Gandy/Peace, creating spaces that delight his clients, and Chris, capturing the essence of those exciting spaces with his photography.

The interior designer sees well-designed spaces as an expression and reflection of who we are and how we live, or, as was portrayed in some classic Hollywood films, as who we'd like to be and how we'd like to live. The photographs in this book give us something to aspire to, because design can, and does, change and shape lives.

Charles explains, in a conversational manner reflective of his warm, humorous sensibilities, why the images Chris captured appeal to our sense of order and appropriateness. The designers featured in this book were not highlighted because they met some cut-and-dried specifications, but because they learned and exercised the fundamentals of design through experience and talent. The author is not interested in pronouncing unbending, unimaginative rules, but in providing inspired and educated guidance.

We can educate our palate for good design by observing examples like the ones found in this book. Learning by seeing is a proven educational technique. Exposure, repeatedly, to quality design, whether in person or through publications, enhances our appreciation and sharpens our eye's ability to discern carefully thought out and well-executed interiors.

So prepare yourself for a visual feast, with a rich dessert of wise and witty observations about the design process. Never will learning be easier or more enjoyable than the time you'll spend in the company of Charles Gandy and Chris Little.

BJ Peterson, FASID
Peterson/Arce Design Group
Former National President of the American Society
of Interior Designers

INTRODUCTION

Design is one of the most powerful forces in our environment. Through design, lives are changed, attitudes are lifted, and dreams inspired. It's no wonder that we are deluged with design ideas. From television series and books to magazines and tours—design, design, design! With so much information, it seems inconceivable that design remains such a mystery to so many. Why are we drawn to watch another television makeover show, peruse another tour of homes, or tear out another magazine page—always in search of novel ideas?

What we're searching for are guiding principles: rules that underlay good design. We live in a world of rules: stop when the light is red, drink white wine with fish, don't wear white after Labor Day. Rules, rules, rules! This need for rules, for order, is what makes the mystery of design so compelling. Unfortunately, there are no hard-and-fast "rules" of design. Instead, design is a search for "good" and "better"—an exercise of trial and error. It is an exploration of learning how to creatively observe, analyze, and then decide, based on certain principles, what solution is good and how it can be improved.

Some may say that good design is timeless. Although at first glance this seems plausible, one realizes upon closer examination that good design is timeless within limits. As times change, so do the "good" and "better" of design.

Take fashion, for example. Few would argue that the clothes worn by the flamboyant King Louis XV were not the best they could be. Made of the finest silks and other exquisite materials and sewn with meticulous care, each garment was a work of beauty, representing a refined aesthetic. Louis's clothes were, no doubt, masterpieces—for their time. But timeless? No! If these garments were timeless, you might see the magnates of Wall Street dressed in such finery today. The way we interpret the basic guidelines of taste and design are in constant flux. The scale, rhythm, proportion, line, balance, and attitude regarding color and texture change with the times.

Beautiful Interiors is presented, therefore, as an evaluation of how these basic principles are manifested in our time. No doubt, style will change—and probably revisit us again! But by understanding some basic rules, you'll always be able to recognize something "good," and know how to make it "better."

Understanding the
FUNDAMENTALS

Where do you start? Easy—at the beginning! It seems so obvious, but how many people do you know who begin decorating by choosing their favorite color, or a favorite chair, or a piece of furniture they think is part of the hottest new trend, and voila!—they start decorating and wonder why the finished scheme doesn't always work. Well, the answer lies in the fact that they don't understand the basics of design.

Like any area of study, interior design requires a foundation—at least a basic one. Without a foundation, you'll have very little chance of succeeding at your endeavor.

What's the first thing you learn in school? The ABCs. Knowing the alphabet makes learning to read and write possible. Decorating is no different: we need to learn—and master—the ABCs of design in order to

decorate well. This book will teach you to understand and speak the basics of design's language.

There are many principles of design and variations and nuances of each. Understanding the terms used to describe them and how they apply to decorating can be as simple or as complex as you choose to make it. Like all of design, there are no real hard-and-fast "rules" for decorating well. Moreover, the principles often overlap or exist as dynamic influences on one another; sometimes, in fact, it's difficult to separate one principle from the other. But knowing how to recognize and apply some basic ideas will help you devise solutions to decorating problems. Likewise, knowing and understanding these terms and principles will make

Above and right: Using all the elements of design, including color, line, scale, rhythm, and others, you can create memorable spaces and tablescapes.

it easier for you to communicate your ideas in a more professional and clear manner to people who can help you achieve the look you're after. As with the ABCs, the more you use them, the easier they become. Thinking about these principles, analyzing them, and using them over and again will soon become second nature and your decorating decisions will become easier and be better for it.

Knowing how to recognize and apply some basic ideas will help you make educated decisions and devise solutions to decorating problems.

Above and left: Whether traditional or contemporary, the whole is always more than the sum its parts.

Page 15: Careful attention to scale, proportion, texture, and color make this living room area warm and comfortable.

Line

The word "line" is one that we use often in design. We talk about the graceful lines of a chair leg, how the lines of a railing work within the context of the stairs, or how the lines of paneling work with the height of the room. Defining "line" can be elusive: in order to understand how to use this design principle in your planning, we need to define the different types of lines and the emotional effect of each.

There are four categories of line that are easy to recognize: horizontal, vertical, diagonal, and curved.

Horizontal Line. A horizontal line, as the word implies, lies parallel to the floor: think of a classic 1950s ranch house that clings to the ground or a sleek contemporary coffee table that floats long and low in front of the sofa. Horizontal lines are usually calmer and less dynamic than other lines; they're also less formal. Consider that coffee table as an example. A simple low rectangular coffee table is less dynamic than a kidney-shaped coffee table—a table that would be better described using the term "curved" line. Pickets in a stair rail that run horizontal are less energetic than the vertical ones. Just think of horizontal line as a human being lying down: calm and quiet.

Vertical Line. Standing proud and tall, vertical lines are bold and active: they resist gravity. Think of a tall building that soars to the sky, an avenue lined with tall and majestic Cyprus trees, or the columns in an ancient cathedral: all force the eye to move upward. Vertical lines add drama and dignity to a space. They also give a room a more formal feel. Bold vertical stripes on wallpaper, a tall vertical mirror in the entry hall, or even the vertical lines of a series of candles on a sideboard help balance the horizontal lines of the floor and furniture. Like a standing human or a soaring sequoia, vertical lines are active and stately. They add strength and vitality to a room.

Page 16: Horizontal lines in the stone and mortar patterns, seating, shelves, and table help to create a serene and stately living space.

Above: Strong vertical lines are formal and dignified.

Diagonal Lines. Less used and less understood than horizontal and vertical lines, diagonal lines are more difficult to use effectively because they are so active (think of a falling tree or a steep mountain slope). My grandmother used to hang three pictures in a diagonal row going up a staircase; she was trying to follow the sloping line of the stairwell, but it never quite worked. Because they're so active and dynamic, diagonal lines are more difficult to control: they keep the eye in constant motion and can create a lack of ease. This is not to say that diagonals can't be used successfully: when used properly they can add energy and power to a room. Just use them sparingly and carefully.

Curved Line. Perhaps the most whimsical of all the lines is the curved line. Think of walking into a space and seeing a spiral staircase—a classic example of strong curved line. Such a staircase adds style and surprise to a room. More playful and less rigid than any of the straight lines discussed earlier, curved lines are soft, flowing, and lyrical. As with diagonal lines, use them cautiously: because they're so active, they can easily overpower a room.

Above: Curved lines in the columns and dropped ceilings offset the strong angularity of this space, making it a much more dynamic room.

Page 18: The curved lines of this dynamic spiral staircase dominate a space filled with horizontal and vertical lines.

Above: A curved, slanted staircase makes a dramatic entry point to a room.

Rhythm

The heartbeat of an interior, rhythm, is a critical element in any space. As the tempo of a beautiful piece of music changes its mood, so does the rhythm of an interior. There are three basic forms of rhythm that bear mentioning: regular rhythm, irregular rhythm, and progressive rhythm.

Regular Rhythm. Like the steady beating of a drum, using regular rhythm in a space adds order and can have a calming effect. Think of a line of equally-spaced votive candles marching like soldiers along a mantel in your living room, or a series of family photographs, each the same size and similarly framed, hanging on your wall. Regular rhythm is a safe and effective design solution, but using it too often can make a room feel static.

Irregular Rhythm. Less formal than regular rhythm, irregular rhythm creates movement (or chaos, if it's not used properly). Consider those family photographs. By mounting them in different sized frames with different finishes and placing them irregularly on the wall, you can create a dynamic presentation for an active family. The sporadic placement of ornaments on a Christmas tree can convey the hectic yet spontaneous joys of the season. Because of its lack of order, irregular rhythm can be more difficult to use effectively than the more staid pacing of regular rhythm. But with practice, this guiding principle can add character and improvisational flair to any space.

Left: Two examples of regular rhythm; an ordered look can be calming.

Page 21: Regular rhythm (the pictures) combines with irregular rhythm (the objects on the sideboard) and progressive rhythm (the pitchers on the shelf) to create a balanced arrangement in this dining room.

Progressive Rhythm. Like diagonal lines, progressive rhythm is harder to use and understand and therefore is not seen as often as regular and irregular rhythm. When used properly and carefully, however, progressive rhythm can add an exciting and dynamic quality to a room. A beautiful cluster of three candles of the same diameter but of three different heights can be beautiful when centered in the middle of a wreath. What's the difference between progressive rhythm and irregular rhythm? Progressive rhythm incorporates anticipation and sequence, while irregular rhythm is random. When you see three stones, each larger than the other, sitting in a row, and you can easily imagine an even larger fourth one being added to complete the sequence, that's progressive rhythm.

Scale

The scale of an element is its size relative to other nearby objects. Perhaps more than any of the other principle of design, the careful use of scale can have an enormous impact on the feeling of a room or space. Like all the other principles, there is no "right" or "wrong" when it comes to using proper scale—finding what works best is a matter of trial and error. But by studying how the relationships of the sizes of the objects make you feel, you can, with time, develop a keen sense of how to balance them. Although large objects tend to be bold, and small ones more delicate, the thing to remember is that scale is always relative: five large objects only appear large in contrast to smaller ones, while smaller decorations may not seem dainty until compared to a large stone statue. Daring to be extreme in scale decisions can make a strong statement in your room. In design, size does matter: it can be a potent tool for your interior.

As the tempo of a beautiful piece of music changes its mood, so does the rhythm of an interior.

Above: Scale in action—a large tapestry dominates a smaller table to create a unique dining space.

Page 22: Red candles march along the mantel in an irregular rhythm, adding playful variety to the room.

Scale is always relative:
five large objects only
appear large in contrast to
smaller ones, while smaller
decorations may not seem
dainty until compared
to a large stone statue.

Above: A large, beautiful painting commands attention.

Right: A boldly scaled mirror accentuates the silver-leafed
and mahogany walls in this sitting area.

Page 25: Large-scale furniture and artwork create a dynamic—but not
overly imposing—composition.

25

Shape

A simple approach to understanding shape is to think of it as two-dimensional: circles, squares, rectangles, ovals, and even odd shapes such as trapezoids and parallelograms can be combined or used alone to convey mood.

Form

Form is similar to shape, but three-dimensional. A square becomes a cube. A circle becomes a cylinder or a sphere. By combining these and other form, you'll have an unlimited palette with which to create any design.

There are four basic types of forms: cubes, cylinders, spheres, and cones.

Cubes. Perhaps the most basic form is the cube. A cube has six equal dimensions, one in each direction. A rectangle can take on a three-dimensional form and become a rectangular cube—a description that is not technically correct but nonetheless useful.

Cylinders. Cylinders, both solid and hollow, are popular forms for interiors. From candles to table legs, cylinders add softness to a room.

Spheres. Perhaps the most universal form, the sphere—again, either solid, hollow, or even partial like a bowl—adds softness and complexity to any space.

Cones. Conical shapes add a dynamic texture to a room by combining the qualities of several forms into one. They tend to be active and directional, leading the eye in the direction of the pointed side.

Left and page 27: Carefully chosen shapes and forms combine to create dynamically balanced settings and tablescapes.

Balance

We can all relate to a balanced budget, or to the balanced scale of justice, or even to the idea of being balanced on a seesaw. Balance in design is no different: one side counterweighs the other, either symmetrically or asymmetrically.

Symmetry. Every time I see a symmetrically designed space or composition, I am reminded of an auction I once attended with a good client and friend. In an ongoing effort by the auctioneer to describe what he was attempting to sell, he would proudly tout the asymmetrical design of the object. My well-informed friend looked at me with a quizzical and knowing look because she knew that what the man was describing was indeed a very symmetrical design—the auctioneer had his terms confused! It has become one of those family jokes whenever either of us hears or sees something symmetrical; we exchange a chuckle and we think of that misguided auctioneer.

It's easy to remember the difference between symmetrical design and asymmetrical design if you remember that symmetry is "safe," which starts with an "s" (the same as symmetrical). Imagine drawing a line down the middle of an object or space. In a symmetrical design, the object is exactly the same on both sides of that imaginary line. Usually safer and more formal, a symmetrical design is a more comfortable and expected solution. It is ordered, proper, and solid.

Top left: A beautifully balanced composition is achieved by combining symmetry and asymmetry, using matching lamps and frames of different shapes.

Left: Symmetrical shelf units stabilize this living room.

Page 29, left: Slight variances between the accessories on the left and right offer a counterpoint in this largely symmetrical composition.

Page 29, right: The console and matching planters bring balance to this entryway. A classical sculpture is placed in front of a contemporary painting that combines symmetrical and asymmetrical elements, making this a unique and interesting ensemble.

Usually safer and more formal, a symmetrical design is a more comfortable and expected solution. It is ordered, proper, and solid.

Asymmetry. By contrast, asymmetrical design is less formal and, although harder to achieve, offers a greater opportunity for individual expression and creativity. Objects on either side of that imaginary line are never the same in an asymmetrical design. Careful attention to the details, scales, and proportions of the various elements on each side ensure good balance.

Sometimes asymmetry is achieved by mistake. I am reminded of a famous mirror that hangs in the dining room of the Swan House, a historically significant museum in Atlanta. I admired that mirror on many visits to the museum before a very knowledgeable docent pointed out that the mirror had a beautiful asymmetrical design. The fabricator of the mirror used a famous pattern book to make it. In an effort to save on paper and print, the publisher of this pattern book drew the various designs with a line down the middle showing two different designs on the same drawing. The intention, of course, was for the maker of the mirror to duplicate either side of this design on the other—a symmetrical design. Wrong! This craftsman very carefully and beautifully duplicated the mirror exactly as it was pictured. The result is a very fine example of asymmetrical design. It is a good thing that the publisher chose two designs that were balanced.

So take a look at your living-room mantel or dining-room buffet. Is the design symmetrical or asymmetrical? If so, would a change be beneficial?

Page 30: Symmetry (matching sconces and chairs) and asymmetry (variety in the tablescape) combine in this classical setting.

Above: Dramatically different-shaped shells and coral bring asymmetry to this otherwise repetitive shelf unit.

Mass

Every object has mass: it can be dense, lightweight, or anywhere in between. There are times that a more dominant mass—that is, a bulkier one—is more appropriate than a lightweight object. Think of a sofa, for example: one with a heavy skirt and bulky arms may be appropriate for one room, but not another. In contrast, a lighter weight sofa—one with lighter mass—with thin horizontal lines might work well in a different room. Choosing an object with appropriate mass depends on the mood you're trying to convey. Do you want to create a stable, cozy room that you sink into, or a wispy, uplifting one that smacks of sophistication? Most people are apprehensive about using a heavier mass; but when used properly, mass can unify and ground your space.

I am reminded of a client who had a very large living-room space with tall ceilings. The clients insisted that their space be intimate and comfortable. A grouping of sofas and comfortable chairs arranged around a massive, solid coffee table brought the room together. In this case, a lightweight glass-topped table would have been less successful; it would have created a floating, airy feel that would have been inappropriate for their needs.

Above, left: The mass of this bulky sofa is counterbalanced by the airy lightness of its matching chair.

Above, right: A massive coffee table anchors an otherwise airy living room.

Right: This example of the bold use of massive objects (wooden knifeboxes, mirror frame, oversized leather chair and ottoman, and thick-legged table) shows how far you can push the envelope and still create a room that's comfortable and inviting.

Texture

Texture is sometimes forgotten in the decorating palette, but it is, without question, one of the most important elements in any space. The texture of an object or wall, whether smooth, rough, stippled, or patterned, adds sensual interest to a room. When used carefully, it can add a subtle—or not so subtle—depth to a space. But be warned: texture is easily overused. How many times have good spaces been ruined with those infamous "popcorn" plaster ceilings? Or consider the mopped-on patterns of textured ceilings, which are usually created to hide bad sheet-rock finishes.

While there is no fault in trying to hide such imperfections, their camouflage can be controlled with a more regular pattern—a texture that works with the space and not against it. Proper use of texture does just that—at best, it complements and enhances a space. In some cases the texture is "the" element; in others, it assumes a more supporting role. In either case, texture is the glue that holds the whole space together; it can make a room feel rich and engaging.

Pattern

Patterns come in a variety of sizes, shapes, colors, and textures. Whether they're large flowers emblazoned on a cotton chintz or vertical stripes on wallpaper, patterns can be bold and definite or simple, quiet, and subtle. What is most important is that you choose a pattern that conveys the mood you're trying to achieve and that it works with the scale, color, shape, and texture of the rest of the objects in the room.

Page 34: Interesting textures contribute to the rugged western atmosphere in this rustic room.

Above and right: Pattern can often soften a room, creating a more romantic or inviting effect.

Closure

Closure is the quality that makes a group of objects in space and time cease to be separate and become a group. Consider a grouping of five framed photographs that you want to hang on a wall. Do you hang them two inches apart, three inches apart, or five inches apart? The answer depends on whether you want the photographs to read as five individual photos or as one group of five photographs. By creating a scaled drawing of the wall and laying out a number of different options for the spacing of these photographs, you can decide which is the best approach to take. As a design student I was once instructed to cut a number of same-size circles from black construction paper and create a series of studies. I and the other students started by gluing five of these circles on the outer edge of an individual white sheet of paper. On the next sheet, we moved the circles in toward the

Above and right: Closure creates unity, as shown in these collections of wall hangings. Multiple objects are read by the eye as a single entity.

center about an eighth of an inch. Then we moved the circles another eighth of an inch. We continued in this exercise until these five black circles were almost touching one another. Once completed, we put this collection of black dots on white paper on the wall and stood back and studied them. It was amazing to see how these five dots transformed from individual objects to a group. At the time, we thought this was a silly exercise. But, after all these years, I remember that exercise more than any other I did in school because I have used the idea of closure as much or more than any of the other principles. With practice, the effective application of closure becomes second nature—and a powerful tool in your design decisions.

Above and right: The principle of closure isn't only applicable to framed artwork. Here, three-dimensional objects and collections become a unified whole.

Variety

We have often heard that variety is the spice of life. Variety is also the spice of any interior. By varying pattern, texture, color, scale, and rhythm, you can add drama and interest to any space. How much variety, of course, is the key. As with spices, you have to be careful how much you add. Too much salt in the pasta will ruin it, and not enough will make it bland. Using all the spices in the cabinet for the same recipe would be overwhelming. The same is true of your interior: some variety is important, too much can ruin a room.

Proportion

The relationship of one object to others in a space, or even to its own properties, is called proportion, and it may be one of the most overlooked principles of design. When considering proportion, you must consider how various elements work together. How does the lamp shade work with the base of the table lamp? Would that shade be in better proportion if it were two inches taller or shorter? What about the lines of the legs of the table in relationship to the skirt or apron of the table? All of the questions relate to proportion. Think of proportion as a ratio: how does one element of an object rate against others in the same piece? The more you observe good and better examples of proportion, the more educated your eye will become and your design

When considering
proportion, you must
think about how
furniture and accessories
work—or don't work—
together.

decisions will be easier. Studying proportion, like all the
other elements, can be as simple as preparing a scaled, detailed
drawing of your room. It is much easier to change the shape or
size of a lamp shade on paper than in reality.

Page 40, left: Pattern and textural variety in action. Note that
the colors in each pattern hold the composition together just
enough to allow the designer to experiment with rich textures.

Page 40, right: The palette in this room brings unity, while
its textural variety adds sensual interest.

Above: The comparable proportion of this chair and loveseat
(along with their similar color) unifies this living room.

Right: The relationship of this mantel and overmantel underscores
the importance of proportion as a unifying force

SETTING THE STAGE

A talented designer friend of mine tells of his memorable design professor who would exclaim: "Walls! Floors! Ceilings! Doors! And windows! That's what makes an interior—nothing more, nothing less!"

I think that professor is right—well, almost right. An interior is the "background" of the room; it sets the stage for its features and overall mood. Defining the interior this way, I would add two attributes to the professor's list: lighting and color. My friend told me that his professor felt that color and lighting were embellishments, but I think they're more integral—even crucial—to an interior.

Like the basic principles and guidelines of design, understanding and mastering the concepts of creating a great background can become second nature if you take the time to consider your options

and opportunities. The key is to become aware of all the details of a room and to realize that every element contributes to the setting. The floors are important. What color are they? What material are they made from? The ceilings are important. What textures do they reveal? Are pipes exposed or hidden? The doors, the walls—every element contributes to how the room feels. Beginners often take certain details for granted and don't take the time to consider how much they add—or detract, if not properly considered—from the whole. Just remember: everything in a room matters. If you want to set the stage, become more sensitive to the details that make it.

Above: Irregular rhythm (shelving) and variations in curved and angular lines (chairs and table) combine to set a perfect "stage" for entertaining.

Right: Soft, botanical fabrics, stencils invoking nature, and closure set a calm, comforting stage for relaxation.

44

Floors

The floor is the base of the interior. What lies underfoot carries important psychological meaning to us—we feel secure if we have solid footing and know what we are walking on. I am reminded of guests who come to my lake house. When pressed for a reason why some dislike swimming in the lake, the answer is invariably that they don't like walking on the spongy algae-covered lake bottom. They don't like that feeling of not knowing what their feet are touching or the insecurity of walking on a less-than-solid surface. The same can be said of our floors—we're not necessarily talking about the actual solidity of the floor (we hope that your home is safe!) but more the *perceived* solidity of the floor. Does it ground the space visually? Does it create a sense of weight in a room? Do you feel comfortable resting your weight on it?

There are dozens of questions to ask yourself about your choice of flooring. Is your floor a focal point of the room or is it simply a quiet foundation? Is the flooring selection appropriate for the location and level of foot traffic you expect in the room? You wouldn't use a soft, fragile carpet for a heavily used hallway, for example. All of these questions and more are important to consider when thinking of the best approach to your floor.

Other alternatives can be intriguing—don't limit yourself to the tried and true! Here are some materials you might not have thought of to dress up your floors:

Concrete. Concrete floors are a great option. When properly installed, these floors can be exotic as well as practical. By adding penetrating stains and waxes, you can create anything from an old-world to a new loft look. Scoring a pattern in the finished concrete floor adds dimension and texture. Concrete floors are easy to maintain and durable for years to come. (Hint: If possible, install a

Page 44 and above: Texture and pattern work together to create impactful floors. Whether a graphical element (the star in the terrazzo at left) or a pattern (the checkerboard above) dominates, the floor always grounds a space.

heating strip under the concrete. These inexpensive heat tapes are thermostatically controlled, use very little energy, and make your concrete floor even more user-friendly.)

Cork. Another great material for the floor, cork is available in rolls or twelve-inch squares in a variety of colors and textures. It provides a unique look and a simple softness underfoot. When properly installed and maintained with an occasional application of paste wax, cork can and should last for years. It's an attractive and often unexpected alternative to other hard-surface materials.

Bamboo. One of the oldest building materials, bamboo is finally showing up on floors. Available in prefinished strips, bamboo offers an exotic alternative to standard oak flooring. The subtle pattern of the bamboo coupled with its durability make it a practical—and beautiful—solution to your flooring problem.

Terrazzo. Terrazzo flooring is not just for retro interiors. Artists working in terrazzo today are taking their patterns and layouts to a new dimension, revitalizing their art and making old material new again. I recently saw a terrazzo installation where the entire floor was covered in overscaled leaf patterns, each leaf three or four feet long. Terrazzos can be bold and exclamatory or delicate and refined...it's all up to you.

Exotic Woods. Wood floors are still a viable solution to flooring, but consider species other than the standard oak. Teak, for example, is a great wood for the floor. A bit more expensive than other possibilities, teak's beautifully textured grain adds rich depth to

Above, right: Special interest can be added to floors when multiple materials are combined. Here, a terrazzo combines with parquet flooring for a simple but dramatic effect.

Page 47: Strong graphical patterns make a bold statement in this living room.

What lies underfoot carries important psychological meaning to us—we feel secure if we have solid footing and know what we are walking on.

There are thousands of options for painting, covering, paneling, texturing, and treating our walls—and each one creates a different effect and elicits a particular emotional response.

Above: Wooden walls adorn this home library, adding a richness and warmth to the classically designed space.

Page 49: Exposed brick walls bearing traces of the building's past contrast with modern furniture to create this dynamic setting. Massive pillars frame the area, while the glass-topped table brings a weightlessness to the center of the room.

surfaces. (Note: It is important to verify that your source of teak is from tree farms, not from endangered forests.)

Just remember: when considering your floors, the sky's the limit! Think creatively, and always keep in mind the mood you're trying to create. The soft, inviting luxury of carpet may be right for you, or perhaps it's the rugged but intimate feel of plank flooring that suits your room. Either way, pay special to your floor; it literally lays the groundwork for the rest of the interior.

Walls

The walls of a space are probably the easiest of all the parts of the interior for us to consider. We are accustomed to thinking about our walls: they're the most obvious starting point when considering the look of a space. How we treat them, therefore, is very important. There are thousands of options for painting, covering, paneling, texturing, and treating our walls—and each one creates a different effect and elicits a particular emotional response. How do you know whether to panel or paint? When do you apply molding? Should you use stone or plaster?

The options seem endless, but we return to our question of appropriateness. Ask yourself, "What is the appropriate solution for what I am trying to accomplish in this space?" What is the room's function? Is it a formal or informal gathering space? By whom will the room be used? Is it appropriate for the room to be dark and cozy or light and airy?

One approach to take when considering the walls of your space is to consider the function of the walls of a room. It seems unnecessary to panel garage walls, but by wallpapering them in heavy vinyl, you've created a practical solution for a heavily used (and often

Left: A ceiling with exposed wooden beams inlaid with graphically painted patterns creates a rustic, cabinlike mood in this living room.

Page 51: Say no to ceiling white! You needn't be Michaelangelo to paint beautiful ceilings. Use your imagination, and be bold!

greasy) area. A bathroom wall needs a more durable surface than the walls of a dining room. A silk wallcovering might work beautifully in the dining room but would be inappropriate in the bathroom. Take the time to consider your options. Think about the use of the room and choose solutions that are appropriate to it.

Ceilings

The next time you enter a new space, look up. The ceiling may offer options you hadn't thought of.

In recent years, ceilings have become little more than a simple plane, most often painted a bland white. Most paint companies even offer a color named "ceiling white." Talk about unimaginative! Historically, however, the ceiling has often played a vital role in interiors. The Sistine Chapel ceiling, for example, is clearly the focal point of its room. And what about the coffered ceilings of old English or French castles, or the wonderful plastered ceilings of so many European rooms?

We in our modern boxes have forgotten to pay attention to this important part of our room. The good news is that it's easy to regain this awareness and use it to our advantage. Adding interest to the ceiling does not have to be difficult or expensive. Paint, for instance, can go a long way in making the ceiling an exciting part of the interior. Imagine a large triangular or harlequin pattern painted on the ceiling. How about an oversized, multicolored target painted on the ceiling of a child's room?

If you're adventurous, try suspending objects from the ceiling. Clouds, mobiles, domes, flags, and other collector's items can draw attention to an otherwise nondescript ceiling. Beamed ceilings also add visual interest. I like to create false sheetrock beams, adding detail to the design and painting them with different values of the same color to create graphical rhythm. Try applying layers of sheetrock to a ceiling: it's a simple and cost-effective way to create

When we touch the molding or trim surrounding a door, when we turn its doorknob or lever, we connect to it more deeply than we do most other objects that make up our interior's background

dimensional effects. Bordering a room with cascading layers of sheetrock can turn a flat ceiling into a sculptural showpiece.

Draping is another effective way jazz up your ceiling. A tented ceiling is romantic (perhaps it brings out the Bohemian in us). It's also an obvious way to hide soiled or unsightly marks overhead.

Doors

God is in the details, and one of the most important details in an interior is the door. Doors play such an important part in underscoring a room's overall feel. When we touch the molding or trim surrounding a door, when we turn its doorknob or lever, we connect to it more deeply than we do most other objects that make up our interior's background. We relate to the scale of doors; we walk though them; they reveal a room to us. They uncover mysteries.

Doors can be practical, separating one space from another. They can be ceremonial. They can say, "Welcome, come in." Think of a gracious hostess swinging open a pair of double doors into a dining room and announcing dinner. Doors can be whimsical—what's more fun than an old Dutch door with the bottom half closed and the top half swung open?

Whether the door is glass (revealing), paneled (formal or rustic), solid-core (dramatic and weighty), or brightly painted (dynamic and fun), the door makes a powerful statement. The door—along with its hardware, trim, and baseboard—creates an overture to a room.

Above: Wrought-iron gates welcome the visitor to this exotic wine cellar. Doors don't have to be solid.

Page 53: A heavy wooden door with custom hardware underscores the spiritual sanctuary of the space.

53

Windows

Like doors, windows carry important psychological meaning—the eyes are often called the "windows of the soul." Besides the practical aspects of letting light into a space, windows add interest and texture to an interior's background. That texture is affected by a variety of factors: the view the window reveals, its covering treatment, its shape, and more.

Too often, the function of windows are not considered. How many times have you seen heavy draperies covering an entire window with a beautiful patch of woods on the other side? This is not to say that one should not use draperies—on the contrary, draperies are often quite important and impactful. Why install a strangely shaped window that will make it difficult to find and hang treatments?

Like all other areas of the interior, scale plays an important role when making window decisions. A window that is too large can dwarf your furnishings and diminish privacy. Windows that are too high or too low can be impractical to wash and can create unwanted lighting effects.

Some important things to consider:

• Keep in mind the way the window opens to the room; this will affect your treatment. Windows that open into the room make it difficult to hang draperies inside. Similarly, a shade or shutter may block an in-opening window.

• Insure the rod extends far enough away from the frame so the window will open (be warned: moving the rod back too far may affect the proportion of the draperies and expose the window frame.

Page 54 and right: Windows, draped or adorned, can bring scale, shape, rhythm, line, pattern, and even color into play.

Above: Recessed, adjustable accent lighting in the soffit spotlights a simply framed, textured painting. Clean lines and asymmetrically placed objects give this area a contemporary look.

Page 57: Lighting fixtures hidden behind a recessed niche illuminate a stone wall and employ repetition and rhythm to add drama.

Lighting

Every time I flip a switch or turn the knob to light a table lamp, I give a silent but grateful prayer to old Thomas Edison for creating the electric light.

Now don't misunderstand, I still love candles. I often light entire rooms (especially dining rooms) with nothing but candles. But can you imagine how expensive and ineffective candles would be in a kitchen, or at your desk when you are working? As romantic and dramatic as candles are, there is certainly no substitute for the reliability of electric light.

Three basic types of lighting are used in an interior: general lighting, accent lighting, and task lighting. How you mix and balance these types depends on your desired effect. By using these three types of light, you can create moods ranging from dramatic to romantic, or anywhere in between.

General Lighting. General lighting allows you to enter a room and find your way in and through it without bumping into furniture. Among the most common forms that general lighting takes is the center-of-the-room overhead lamp. I often avoid this kind of general illumination because it's so commonplace (although a beautiful and appropriately chosen chandelier or hanging fixture can anchor a room). If I do use an overhead fixture in the center of a room, I generally keep it dimmed; if a dimmer is not available, I use a very low-wattage lamp (the proper word for "bulb").

Some rooms require more general lighting than others. A kitchen, for instance, will benefit from a lot of light (you do, after all, need to be able to see to cook and clean up). But don't forget the dimmer! It's nice to tone the light down a bit, especially if you are eating in the kitchen. Likewise, bathrooms need a lot of general illumination.

Above: Lighting beside a bed or chair makes reading easy and enjoyable while adding to the beauty of your arrangement.

Page 59: Recessed accent lighting illuminates this dramatic artwork.

But general illumination alone makes for an uninspired space. Here are some other ways to light up a room.

Accent Lighting: Accent lighting highlights specific parts of your space, adding a secondary sparkle to a room. Table lamps, sconces, picture lights (recessed or wall-mounted), torchières, and yes, even candles, are examples of this versatile interior element. I often will use accent lighting (all on dimmers, of course) as my general light source, letting the "spill" light from these fixtures fill the room. One way to control or "build" light in a room is to plug half of your fixtures into a switchable outlet, so that you can flip a switch when you enter the room and provide enough light to negotiate the furniture. You can then control the mood of the room by individually turning on the fixtures you want to.

The variety of accent fixtures you can choose from is endless. So is the number of lamps, each with its unique beam spread and color quality. You have many opportunities to have a dramatic lighting plan.

Task Lighting. Task lighting, as the name implies, helps you perform a specific function. The reading fixture beside your bed or on your desk, or the magnifying fixture that helps you see your needlepoint project or put on your makeup, are all examples of task lighting.

As with all aspects of design, the key question to ask yourself is, "What mood am I trying to create?" Do you want to heighten drama (by using bright directional light, for example) or calm the room down (using diffused, or indirect, light)? Do you want to create an atmosphere of intimate romance (with candles) or bold energy (by using bright-colored lampshades)? Just remember what your needs are, and balance your light sources to meet them.

Color

Complex books hundreds of pages long have been written on the use of color for interiors. Here, we'll keep it simple. Colors evoke emotional responses. Certain colors stimulate, others calm. Some heighten awareness and lift mood, while others fade into the background. In any event, color is among the most powerful tools in creating an interior.

Red is often considered the most stimulating color—it excites the eye and draws attention to itself (statistically, red cars get more speeding tickets than any other kind of car.) Perhaps because of its primordial association with blood and fire, red implies urgency and dramatic importance: emergency and exit signs, sirens, fire trucks, stop signs, and ambulances all make abundant use of the color red. This doesn't mean that one should avoid using red for one's interior. It simply means that one should be aware of its strong impact.

Conversely, color can be calming. Green is often used in hospital and waiting rooms to relax patients and their families. A red room is just as clean as a green one, but somehow the idea of lying ailing in a bright red room doesn't seem nearly as healing as recovering in a space painted sea-foam green.

Color can sculpt forms within a space or change the perceptions of the actual scale or size of a room. Painting the end wall a dark hue, for example, can dramatically shorten a long corridor. Ceilings can appear to be lowered or raised by changing their color. A space can be enlarged or made smaller using only the power of paint.

The psychology of color is real. A major manufacturer of laundry powder once did a test to determine the best color to make their detergent. The basic product was white—snow-white, of course. The solid white product reportedly cleaned the clothes quite well.

When yellow crystals were added to the same detergent, it was said to diminish the effectiveness of the detergent. In contrast, blue crystals were perceived to enhance the detergent's performance. Although the crystals had no actual effect on the cleanliness of the clothing, they had a marked effect on the *perception* of cleanliness in people's minds.

But don't let all this talk of color discourage you from experimenting in your home—it's easy (and not usually expensive) to make a huge difference in the mood of a room by changing its color. With the stroke of a brush, you can change how you—and everyone else—feels when entering your space.

Using Color and Color Schemes

One of the most often asked questions I hear is, "Which colors work well together?" The answer is not that simple: many colors work together, but learning how they do is the subject of thick and scholarly works on color theory. There are, however, some basic principles that will give you at least an introductory glimpse into this fascinating subject.

There are three basic, or primary, colors: red, blue, and yellow. When mixed, the secondary colors emerge: red and blue make violet (or purple), blue and yellow make green, and yellow and red make orange. Tertiary colors result from mixing secondary colors.

Hue is the basic color itself (red or blue, for example). You can change the *tint* of a hue by adding white and the *shade* of the hue by adding black. Likewise, you can make a basic hue more neutral by mixing it with its complementary color (the color that falls directly opposite on the color wheel).

When we think about using color in our interior, we're most often talking about a color scheme. There are three basic types of color schemes: complementary, analogous, and monochromatic.

• **Complementary color schemes** are easy and usually safe. Using a color's complement makes both colors more emphatic. Think about the red and green of Christmas ornaments: each color is brighter and stronger against the other than either one is on its own. A striking example of the effective use of complementary colors has been made by Disney. The next time you go to Disney World, look at the grass; it looks so green. Why? The sidewalks are painted a faded red.

• **Analogous color schemes** use two or three colors that lie adjacent to one another on the color wheel. Think about an analogous scheme of warm yellows, oranges, and reds in a ski lodge or the blue-green palette of a beach-front home. Each uses colors in close proximity on the color wheel.

• **Monochromatic color schemes** use one hue for most elements of the interior. Monochromatic schemes are often confused with *monotone* schemes, which use the same *exact* color for detailing and accenting. Monochromatic schemes use tints and shades of the same color, along with a variety of textures and materials, to add variety and visual interest to a space. Monotone schemes are usually boring and difficult to make work; use variety to your advantage. By using a variety of textures and values, you can achieve a harmonious and sophisticated look using only one hue. Accenting with monochromatic color schemes is easy: you can either stay with the chosen color or break the pattern with

It's easy (and not usually expensive) to make a huge difference in the mood of a room by changing its color. With the stroke of a brush, you can change how you—and everyone else—feels when entering your space.

dramatic results. Adding a brightly colored throw pillow or a vase full of flowers brings visual interest and an unexpected break for the eyes.

The bottom line with using color is to become aware about how it makes you feel and decide if that's appropriate for your room. The good news is that changing the color of your room is inexpensive and fun to do; just be sure to cover the furniture!

Above: A white background emphasizes the vivid color and intrigue of whimsical objects, while the repetition of line contributes to the calming effect of the white walls.

Right: Strongly monochromatic but liberally accented with color, this room shows that color schemes are made to be broken.

EMBELLISHMENTS

Once you've set the stage for your space with the big-ticket items of your interior background, you can begin to embellish it. This is a great opportunity to make your space not only beautiful, but personal and functional.

Embellishing is one of the most enjoyable aspects of creating any interior. It's fun to look at fabrics and furniture, to sit in chairs, to put your feet up on a comfy ottoman and stretch out on the sofa. But like any complicated process, embellishing a room can be a bit overwhelming: there are so many options to choose from. There's also the commitment factor; choosing a paint color doesn't feel quite so final as choosing a sofa. After all, you can easily and relatively inexpensively change the color of your walls if you don't like the result. Changing a sofa can be more costly.

That said, remember that this is the fun part of your work. Take a deep breath and remember that there really are no mistakes—although some decisions are better than others! Once you're armed with a solid understanding of the basic principles of design (the same ones that helped you create your interior background), you can approach the embellishment process with little fear.

A little homework helps in the process as well. In this day and age, we're lucky to have so many opportunities to educate ourselves about the design process. There is a plethora of magazines, books, and television shows that offer examples of how you can embellish your space. Studying these sources with a critical eye will help you find what you're attracted to. It's a great idea to keep a "tear file" of design ideas that you like). But be warned: just because you see an interior in a magazine doesn't mean the design is worthy of repeating. Editors are careful about selecting what they publish, but most are not designers. They are often not prepared (or inclined) to make critical decisions about what works or doesn't work in an interior.

Above and right: Embellishing a room is one of the most fun—and challenging—aspects of decorating. From pillows and fixtures to candlesticks, accessories make a room your own.

Collect photographs of what you like **and** what you don't like. The more you look at these examples, the more you have to help you shape your own ideas.

Above: Furniture is an important embellishment in a room. It can also set a stage for your favorite objets d'art.

Right: Embellishments should work together as a family; here, the organic quality of the feather and orchid relate to the detailing in the chairs and drapery patterns.

Nonetheless, even bad examples of design offer learning opportunities, including the chance to confirm your own aesthetic—they give you a chance to think about what works for you. Collect photographs of what you like *and* what you don't like. The more you look at these examples, the more you have to help you shape your own ideas.

In addition to studying photographs of interiors, it is also important to learn to plan. Making scaled drawings is a great way to begin to make decisions based on more than just reaction. Don't panic—it's not necessary for you to become an architectural draftsman. You can easily learn to make simple scaled drawings. They don't need to be works of art suitable for framing. They are merely studies of how you want to lay out your space. It's a lot easier to move a sofa around on paper than in reality.

Begin these drawings by making a floor plan—a bird's-eye view of what your room looks like. Here are some tips:

• When indicating where doors, windows, and other architectural elements are, include the direction in which they swing open. You'll have a much better idea of which ideas can be dismissed out-of-hand and which ones warrant further study.

• Pick a scale at which to draw and use it consistently. The standard scale for most interiors is either one-quarter inch or one-eighth inch for every foot. That simply means that every quarter inch drawn on the paper represents one foot of actual space. Office supply stores offer bound pads of scaled gridded paper in quarter–inch squares. By deciding that each of these squares equals one or two feet, you have determined that your chosen scale is one–quarter inch or one-eighth inch.

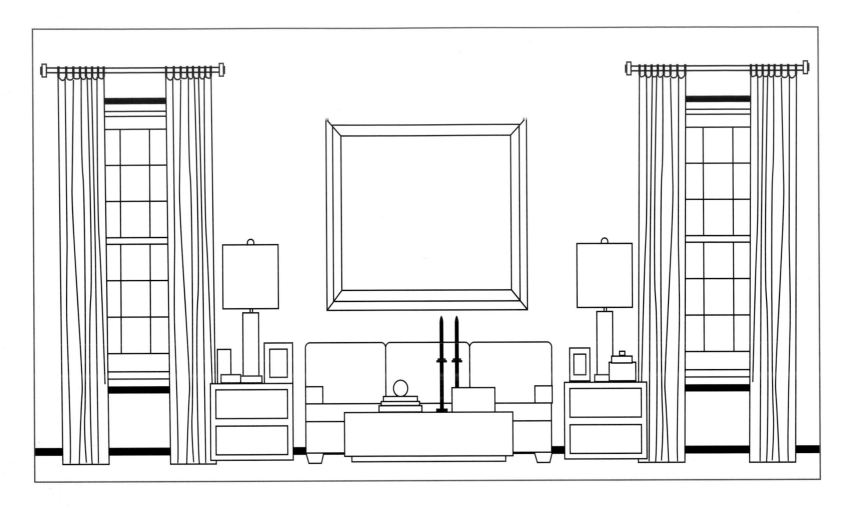

• Once you have drawn the plan, including all the architectural elements, use sheets of tracing paper (also available at the office supply store) to experiment with different furniture layouts using the same base plan.

Drawing a plan may be enough, but to really understand your finished space, draw elevations as well. An elevation is side view of a room with all its elements drawn flat against the it. Elevations are important to understand how the scale of the furniture you have selected works in a space—how it relates to the ceiling heights and to the other furniture in the room. Your eye can fool you—if you look at two photographs of a chair and a sofa, you might think that they are the same basic scale and will work together. This is not

always the case. It's well worth your while to take a few minutes and draw an elevation of your room. Check the relative arm heights, proportions, and scale of one piece to another. Study the mass of each piece and how it relates to the whole room.

Prepared with ideas, photographs, plans, and elevations, you are ready to make the room of your dreams. Selecting furniture is the first step to embellishing a room so it feels like the special space you want and deserve.

Above: An elevation, or scale drawing, helps you compare the relationship of objects in a room without ever lifting a sofa or drilling a hole.

Right: Studying elevations prior to installation helped to ensure proper proportion of the accessories in this tablescape.

Furniture

No interior is complete without furniture, though some rooms have less furniture than others (much of this depends on the style you like: Asian–inspired rooms, for example, require minimal furniture use). Though there are many things to consider when thinking about furniture, decisions all involve two ideas: selection and arrangement.

Selection. Since its earliest days, humankind has been producing furniture—chairs to sit on, tables to eat at, beds to sleep in. The look of furniture has evolved primarily based on three factors: function, scale, and aesthetics. Each of these factors influences your decisions about what furniture is appropriate for your design solution.

For instance, if you need chairs on which to sit and eat, your selection will depend on several factors. Will you eat at a counter on a kitchen island or at a table with a low-lying apron? Will the chairs need arms? If they have arms, should the arms be set back from the front edge of the chair?

These functional decisions are important, but function alone is not enough to make your buying decision—scale also plays a part. Will the chairs be used primarily for adults or children? If you have a thick, bulky, country-style table, you'll also want equally sturdy, large-scale seating—not delicate and spindly wicker chairs.

Aesthetics are also important. Choosing chrome or walnut chairs will depend on your aesthetic approach to the remainder of the room. More subtly, the hardware for one piece of furniture might be more appropriate for your room's mood than another.

Left: The table above is light and angular for a contemporary look, while the chest of drawers below is massive and employs curved lines for an older, classical look.

Opposite: Circular tables provide a powerful contrast to the striped upholstery adorning the unmatching chairs in this room.

Some functional decisions are obvious. A bedroom, of course, needs a bed (a king-sized bed, a queen-sized, a twin?) and a place for your clothes (a closet, shelves, or an armoire?), but other decisions will be based on your lifestyle and preferences. Do you want to pay your bills in the bedroom or in the kitchen? Will you work at home? Where do you like to get ready for work—in the bathroom, the bedroom, or both? Does clutter make you nervous or comfortable? Asking yourself these questions up front will save you a lot of time and money in the long run. Too often, we don't take the time to consider our individual lifestyles and ask the questions that will allow us to make good decisions. Take the time to think about how you like to live, then choose your furnishings accordingly.

Arrangement. How you lay out your furniture in the room is as important as the selection of the pieces. As with selection, the arrangement of furniture depends mostly on practical concerns. Traffic patterns are important to consider—how will you use the room? How will you walk through it? Another is the role the room plays in the context of the home—is it a room for quiet contemplation or social gathering? Once again, analyze your expectations of a room and its function before you sit down and arrange your furniture, and don't forget to use your tracing paper and floor plan.

In placing furniture, function alone is usually not enough to create impact—creativity can make a big difference. Furniture placement is an easy way to change a room with minimal effort. Moving your furniture away from the wall can create a more open, airy feeling in a room. "Floating" your sofa in front of the fireplace can allow traffic

Page 72: Placement of furniture can make quite a difference in the mood of a room. The intimacy of this setup is enhanced by moving the sofa away from the wall, closer to the coffee table and chair.

Right: The space between furniture is a compositional element in both of these rooms. Where you place furniture—and where you don't—controls the energy of the room.

to move behind it and change the character of a space. Flanking the fireplace with two love seats can make a great setting for lively conversation among guests. Adding a table behind the sofa creates a convenient surface for lamps and other decorative items.

We all fall into patterns about how our furniture should be placed—don't be afraid to try something different. Here are some ideas to shake up your space:

• *Get away from the walls.* My bed is in the middle of the room. This unusual placement makes a unique statement (and is certainly a conversation starter!)

• *The ninety-degree solution.* Putting a work desk perpendicular to the wall makes the room come alive—and think about how much nicer it is to face into the room instead of looking at the wall!

• *Furniture can be a wall.* I placed a large armoire at the end of a long corridor that opened into a living/dining room. By upholstering the back of the armoire, I created a surface for an important piece of artwork. This unusual use of the armoire accomplished several things: it provided a focal point at the end of the corridor, a different flow to the traffic entering the room, and a surface on which to place a painting.

The key is to experiment. Move your furniture and be creative. Search for better solutions by trying different options. And if your latest attempt doesn't work, just move it back!

Right, above: Creative placement makes the seating in this room an unexpected focal point.

Below: Another unexpected seating solution—chairs set at odd angles give this room a sense of movement without being chaotic.

Page 75: The bed in this small bedroom floats in its middle. An overscaled mirror leans against the wall, increasing the perceived size of the room.

Fabrics

Choosing the correct fabric can make or break a room, and careful attention to detail makes the difference. Like choosing furniture, selecting fabrics is a matter of function and aesthetics.

Function. Thinking of the end use of any room makes choosing the proper fabric easier. That seems like common sense, but when you see how some people choose fabric, you'll wonder if common sense played any part in the decisions made. Why, for instance, would one choose velvet or some other delicate fabric in a high-traffic multipurpose family room? A heavy woven fabric, perhaps with a colorful pattern, would be a far more practical solution. Leather is versatile and durable, but water will stain it. Why use leather chairs in a kitchen?

Choosing the correct fabric can make or break a room, and careful attention to detail makes the difference.

Above: A classic contemporary ottoman floats unexpectedly in front of a beautiful chest of drawers, offering both additional seating as well as another place for books and reading material.

Left: The durable but soft "hand" of this sofa's fabric make it both comfortable and durable.

Page 77: With its variety of textured fabrics, this stately living room is a visual—and tactile—feast.

Understanding some basic ideas about fabric construction will make decision-making easier. Here are some words to add to your fabric vocabulary:

Warp and Weft. Most fabrics for interior use are woven. The density of the finished fabric will depend on the *warp* (vertical threads) and *weft* (horizontal threads interlaced within the warp) used in the construction of the woven fabric. A 300-count linen sheet, for instance, is a far finer and more delicate fabric than a 200-count sheet (*count* refers to the number of threads per square inch used in the construction).

Denure. The thickness of the thread used. Denure will affect the finished product. A thick bulky thread, for example, will result in a thicker, bulkier finished fabric.

Hand. The quality of how the fabric feels when touched (velvet, for instance, has a distinctly softer hand than a heavily textured cotton twill). How do you want the surface to feel?

Aesthetics. Function alone shouldn't dictate your fabric decisions. Aesthetics are equally, if not more, important. What will the fabric feel and look like? What mixture of fabrics will you have in the space? All of these factors should be considered in your decision.

The texture of fabric is one of the most underrated (and overlooked) factors in a room's character. Two similarly colored fabrics in radically different textures impart entirely different spirits to a room (think of red canvas versus red velvet). A shiny silk fabric will make a formal statement, while a heavy burlap would make a more casual one.

Fabric is also one of the easiest ways to add color to a room. With the unlimited number of color options and patterns available, you'll never run out of ways to express yourself. Just remember to make decisions based on how a fabric works (or does not work) within the context of a room.

Page 78: Brilliant floral fabrics give a visual cue to the wall and window treatments in this elegant room.

Above: Fabrics create sensual interest in a room.

The most practical way to
decide what (if anything)
to do with the window is
to simply look at—
and through—it.

Above: A combination of contrasting treatments—loosely constructed roman shades and full-length traverse draperies—provide an elegant treatment for this sunroom.

Page 81: Beautifully designed and fabricated valances hang over these draperies, giving the room a sophisticated look.

Window Treatments

How (or if) you treat your windows is a major embellishing decision that will greatly affect the rest of your space. The most practical way to decide what (if anything) to do with the window is to simply look at—and through—it. Ask yourself the following:

- Is the window intrinsically attractive? Is it worth featuring and celebrating? Or does it need to be hidden?

- What is outside the window—a delightful view that needs to be championed or an eyesore that needs to be hidden?

- What kind of light enters the room? Does it need to be blocked or screened?

All of these decisions and more need to be made to determine what kind of treatments will work best.

Soft and Hard Window Treatments. Generally, window treatments "soften" the window and make the finished space more comfortable. But window treatments can also be "hard." Shutters, screens, and blinds generally offer a more definitive statement of privacy. Sometimes used in combination with softer coverings, hard window treatments offer a variety of opportunities. Shutters, for example, can hide built-in pockets on the side of heavily set windows.

Hardness is relative, even within the hard window treatment category. Small-slatted shutters are softer than large plantation-type shutters (remember our old friends, scale and proportion). Old-fashioned wooden venetian blinds (either painted or natural) are softer than modern metal blinds.

A more common window treatment is the soft variety, frequently referred to as draperies—not *drapes*. I once had a professor who said "drapes" was a cow's disease. Whether or not that is true, it certainly impressed me. Draperies are very important to any interior. They soften the space, affect the room's acoustics, and add the finishing touch that makes such a difference in a room. Like most of what you've already read about, there are copious options for soft window treatments. Curtains are a lightweight, sometimes unlined option. Sheers, or casements, are often gauzy and loosely draped.

Overtreatments are important to consider as well. Valances, for example, come in a multitude of variations (they're often confused with cornices—valances are soft treatments; cornices are hard). Perhaps the most common valance is a simple panel of fabric with inverted box pleats at the corners. On the other hand, a valance may consist of a series of swags or loosely folded layers of fabric that swoop across a window in waves. These swags may have only one segment and be framed at the sides with cascades—loose vertical folds that fall down the sides. Occasionally a pair of swags is finished with a jabot—a cone-shaped fabric in the middle of the swags. Any or all of these valances can be enhanced with fringe or trim, a contrasting border, or other decorative treatments. Just remember: the trim should not dominate the overall treatment—it should enhance it.

Cornices also come in a number of variations. A straight upholstered cornice is most common. If such a cornice extends down the sides of the window, it becomes a lambrequin. Add curved and upholstered corners, and it is known as a "dog-eared" cornice. Not all cornices are upholstered; some of the most beautiful cornices are wooden, usually carved in a heavy ornate treatment or perhaps in a

Draperies...soften the space, affect the room's acoustics, and add the finishing touch that makes such a difference in a room.

Above: Heavy velvet draperies—finished with an ornate fringe and beautifully elaborate finials—illustrate how a simple tieback can affect a window treatment.

Page 82: The slight curve of the window is celebrated by the rich draperies that traverse to follow it. Notice how the shape of the valance highlights its pattern.

simple detail that mimics the molding in the room. A stylish overtreatment is a combination of a board trim or cornice, under which a soft valance is suspended.

Hardware. A major part of any window treatment is the hardware. Drapery hardware can be as decorative as your space demands. In some cases, the hardware can be almost as important as the fabrics and trims themselves. Decorative tiebacks, rods, and finials come in endless possibilities. I know of one manufacturer that specializes in just finials.

Because there is so much decorative hardware available, I am amazed how often I see the common traverse draperies on an exposed ceiling-mounted rod with the old-fashioned pull cord on the side. Be more creative!

By using your imagination, you can add great character and charm to your window treatments. Take a child's room, for instance. Why not create fun window treatments by using sports equipment as drapery tiebacks? Think about a tennis racket, as an example, that is mounted away from the wall and holds back a "drapery" made of a tennis net! Or, how about using a couple of baseball bats as "rods" with pinstriped draperies hung from rawhide (like the kind used in baseball gloves) through grommets? Other found objects can be used for drapery hardware as well. One of the most successful drapery rods I ever used was a small tree limb in a rustic ranch in Montana. This limb was planed smooth enough to allow the iron rings that held the burlap draperies to slide easily along the rod. It was mounted with rusted antique railroad spikes. The treatment was simple but very effective and quite appropriate in this rustic setting.

A creative friend of mine fashioned finials with personal meaning by incorporating celestial bodies, which always intrigued him. He built a metal sun, moon, and stars—all in different shapes—to serve as finials in his bedroom. The fact that no two finials matched made the treatment very special and added personal interest.

In some cases, you may decide that seeing no hardware is the best solution. Creating a cornice board or valance can dress up an otherwise plain drapery rod. Extending the moldings and baseboard can also be very effective. You can create a tailored effect that hides any rod by taking the same molding that runs along the base and turning it up along the side and above the window.

The bottom line is to make sure you consider the hardware when deciding on any window treatment. It is an essential element that can give your space character.

Above: A heavy, gilded curtain rod adds a regal touch to this setting.

Page 85: A heavy valance with jabots and fringe contrasts with a sheer and lightweight shade.

SPECIFIC SPACES

Homes today are often built similarly. Most have a predictable series of rooms that vary little in kind, regardless of their arrangement in the architectural plans: the same entry halls, living rooms, dining rooms, and the like are found in almost every home. It's important, therefore, to spend some time thinking about these rooms to develop a good understanding of the function of each and how it relates to the house as a whole.

Balancing the individual needs of a room and the needs of the house—seeing the two as one unified entity—

is the key to successful design. Each room must stand alone as an expressive and individual statement but also as part of the greater whole.

What unifies a home? Is it color? Is it using the same carpet throughout the space? Is it a repeating detail such as a crown molding or baseboard? Or is it a style or look of furniture? It can be any one of these concepts, often in combination, or something completely different. The key is that there be something—or, more often, several things—making a space feel like one coherent whole, not a series of disjointed rooms.

How do you unify a home, yet still give each room its own identity? The answer lies in finding balance among the disparate elements that make up the house.

Above: The embellishments you choose—unusual lamps, hand-turned pottery, textured throw pillows—tell your guests who you are.

Right: Pattern and color tie this space together and add to a formal atmosphere.

Entry Halls

Entry halls serve a very important role in your house: they welcome your guests. There is something gracious about stepping into a grand entry and being greeted by your hosts, exchanging pleasantries, and anticipating what's to come in the rest of the house.

How do you accomplish this? One way is to pay close attention to scale. Is your space large and open (a loft, for example) or small and intimate? If it's large enough, try placing a grand table to set the stage dramatically. Tablescaped with family photos, a large bouquet of flowers, or seasonal decorations, an entry table is a fine way to greet company with a warm hello.

Don't have a family heirloom that is worthy of the entry? A simple plywood table draped with your favorite fabric and covered with a thick piece of glass works nicely. When you want a new look, simply change the tablecloth. Remember, if you make your own table,

you can make it the size and shape that best fits your entry. Be creative—not all tables are rectangular! Try organic shapes or geometric ones like octagons and ovals. Why not try nested tables? Let your creativity flow and make your entry table your own.

What if you have an intimate entry hall where there is simply no room for a large table? Try using a smaller pedestal with a great piece of sculpture or a narrow console. How about a pair of consoles with large mirrors above, or a wall-mounted ledge? A small room doesn't have to have small furniture and accessories. In some cases, large-scaled furniture in an intimate space makes the space feel grander.

If you don't have a designated entry hall, create one. It will not only make your guests feel welcome, but it will probably make you happier too. There's nothing better than arriving at home sweet home! Here are some ideas to jumpstart your creativity:

• If your entrance room is big enough, try adding a low wall or a screen that defines an area as the entry.

• Add columns and drop a soffit above them to create an entry within the space.

• Suspend an iron rod from the ceiling and add double-sided draperies.

• Suspend a lightweight fabric from the ceiling to create a canopy effect that separates it from the rest of the living room.

• Try placing a pedestal and sculpture at the entryway.

• Place your living room sofa with its back to the entry door with a table behind it.

• If you have electrical power wired to the center of the floor, you can place two lamps on a sofa table, adding another element of style to help you define the space.

Above: Abundant light makes this entry hall a welcoming one.

Page 89: A draped table floats in the middle of a gracious entry hall. The tailored skirt with its kick pleats and heavy fringe is a great way to say "come in."

Entry halls serve a very important role in your house: they welcome your guests. There is something gracious about stepping into a grand entry and being greeted by your hosts, exchanging pleasantries, and anticipating what's to come in the rest of the house.

Living Rooms

Living rooms are often the most misunderstood—or, more properly, misnamed—rooms in a house. How many times do people create these special living rooms and never go in them? More often than not, the living room is a showpiece. I remember one client who called this room the "preacher's room" because he knew that the only time that the room would probably ever be used was when the preacher came to visit.

For some reason, living rooms often become formal presentation rooms—not that there's anything wrong with formality. There is something nice about having a place where you know you are to be on your best behavior. Some of us can remember being a child and knowing that if you were in the living room, you had to watch your manners. But making a room formal doesn't mean it has to be stuffy and uninviting.

Here are some ideas to make your living room a *living* room:

- **Cut down on the showpiece factor by having your living room serve multiple functions.** In the interest of saving space, many people make the living room double as a home office or library. Such applications not only make the home more efficient, but give it the feeling of being more lived in.

- **Establish a clear focal point.** Is there something special in your room around which the furniture would work well? A fireplace, a beautiful view, or a special painting on a large wall?

Top: A fireplace can provide a focal point or a romantic backdrop in a living room.

Middle: The placement of two sofas define distinct spaces within the room.

Bottom: Conversation is encouraged when seats face each other.

What is the one thing that makes your room special and can be highlighted with your furniture arrangement?

What is the one thing that makes *your* room special and can be highlighted with your furniture arrangement?

- **Consider the traffic patterns of the room.** How will people walk through your space? Would moving the sofa away from the wall create a better traffic pattern? Remember, it is not essential that you make the traffic pattern the most direct. In some cases laying the traffic patterns out so that you move around and through the furniture may be more interesting.

- **Position your chairs and sofas to encourage good conversation.** How many people do you usually entertain? Is there a way to add flexibility to your layout by providing chairs that can pivot to be part of one group or another?

All of these considerations are important to ensure that your furniture is positioned in a way that makes your room inviting and functional. A little effort and thought will indeed make your living room more useable and more livable.

Left: Focal point in this room is shared by an abstract painting and a classical fireplace.

Right: This setting was made for talking! Place your chairs to encourage conversation.

Dining Rooms

Whether casual, formal, or somewhere in between, the dining room is a place where memories are made.

Yet few of us eat in the dining room on a regular basis. In today's fast-paced world, we'll often use the breakfast room or kitchenette (or the table in front of the TV) rather than sitting down for a formal meal. For most people, sitting down to discuss the day's events is, unfortunately, a thing of the past. This fact makes the role of the dining room even more crucial, for on those rare occasions when we do sit together as a family at a beautifully set table, our meal becomes an event.

The dining table plays a critical role in this special room, and our lifestyle is affecting its shape and design. Round tables have once again become popular (some with old-fashioned lazy Susans), as have square tables. Compared to long, rectangular tables, these shapes are more intimate and encourage a less formal (and less hierarchical) seating arrangement.

Some other thoughts to keep in mind:

• Don't forget mirrors! Large mirrors make attractive displays in a dining room. Add a few candles and you are set for your special event.

• Sideboards and servers offer numerous possibilities for making your dining room special. An open Parson's table or console can be most effective if storage is not a problem. A draped table with a thick glass top is always an elegant and relatively inexpensive way to dress up a dining room.

Above: The overscaled painting in this room creates a serene ambience.

Below: Fabric covered walls and molding bring formality to this dining room.

Pages 93-94: Regularly placed chairs, candles, window treatments, and paintings bring calming rhythm to these dining rooms.

Dining Room Chairs. Choosing dining chairs may be one of the most important decisions you make in your decorating scheme. More than just a place to sit, dining chairs dominate the room and dramatically affect its spirit. Take your time and consider all your options, and ask yourself lots of questions. Will you have all side chairs, all armchairs, or some combination? Will the host and hostess have their own kind of chair? Should your chairs be fully upholstered? How tall should they be? Some daring souls make every chair completely different from the next—a collection of chairs. This approach is especially good for young couples just starting out, and it adds a special character to any dining room.

Dining experiences are more than just eating experiences. If you're like I am, you spend as much (or more) time sitting at the table after the meal talking as you did eating. It's important, therefore, that your dining chairs provide the proper level of comfort to encourage this prolonged and important conversation.

The height of the chair plays a large part in setting the stage for conversation. The famous architect and designer Frank Lloyd Wright knew this better than most. His dining chairs were usually quite tall and, when surrounding the table, virtually created a room within a room. This made the table itself a cozy and inviting space for lively conversation.

When selecting a dining chair, it is very important for you to stand away from it and look at it from the rear. When you walk into a dining room, you see the backs of the chairs lined up around the table. First impressions do make a difference, so be sure and check out how your potential chair will look as you approach it from behind.

One point that is often overlooked when selecting a good dining chair is its weight. How easily will the chair slide in and out from under the table? This seemingly minor point becomes more important as we get older. Be careful that your chairs are not so heavy that you and your guests will not be able to move them.

Dining chairs are complicated pieces of furniture. Taking time to make the right selection will be well worth the effort.

Pages 95–97: Dining rooms come in all manner of sizes, shapes, and colors. So do dining chairs. Don't forget to look at the back of a dining chair when making a selection—you'll see it more than any other part of the chair.

Kitchens

Whether traditional or contemporary, the kitchen has become one of the most important rooms in the home today. Accordingly, the same attention to detail made throughout the home is needed in the kitchen.

Having a large and open kitchen is certainly not a new idea—the idealistic image of endless counter space, large-scale appliances, and bountiful natural light remains prominent in many people's minds. But it wasn't always so; changing economies, wars, cultural shifts, and lifestyle changes have moved kitchens from the periphery of the home (where fire couldn't damage the family valuables) to its center. With that move has come a change in the expectation of the room's decor. A kitchen now must not only function as a food-preparation area, but must be as presentable as any other room of the house.

With the advent of kitchen cabinetry that looks like furniture, you can have inviting and beautiful spaces that are also functional. Refrigerators, dishwashers, and other appliances are now available with fronts that match cabinetry. Sophisticated stovetops almost disappear into the counter, while freezers can be hidden in pullout drawers. Pantries and broom closets can be outfitted like fancy wardrobes.

Kitchen islands are wonderful elements that help define spaces within a kitchen. But be warned: don't let your island become so large that it dominates the space. Consider making the island double-tiered with a lower working counter on the kitchen side and a higher eating ledge on the side that opens to the common area.

Pages 98–99: In these examples, cabinetry is sophisticated and well-constructed (almost indistinguishable from millwork in the more formal rooms of the house), chairs are appointed like fine furniture, and countertops are arranged like tablescapes.

A kitchen must not only function as a food-preparation area, but must be as presentable as any other room of the house.

When planning a kitchen, don't forget the ceiling! Changing ceiling planes within a large space is a relatively simple way to define the various functional areas while simultaneously creating ambience. Something as simple as adding a molding or dropping a short soffit around or over an island may be all that is necessary to set off one part of your open kitchen from the other. The ceiling is also a great place to incorporate color into an otherwise drab room. Many appliances and cabinets are only available in neutral and muted tones. Painting the ceiling is a great way to liven up the room inexpensively.

Furniture in open kitchens can be creative as well. Consider replacing the expected dining or breakfast table with large over-stuffed chairs and a tall coffee table that doubles as a dining and game table. Such an informal seating and dining opportunity in the kitchen may even encourage you to use your formal dining room more often.

Bedrooms

Bedrooms are personal, private spaces that should be designed with care to ensure that they meet your many expectations. A delicate balance must be struck between form and function in this important room: since the bedroom is a place for both mental and physical rest, it should be both comfortable and calming to the eye and mind.

The bedroom has other functions as well: it may be the site of a special romantic evening, or a place to heal when one is ill. For many, it's their favorite place to read.

Some of the success of a bedroom depends on the spaces that are adjacent to it. A bedroom that has a separate walk-in closest with built-in storage will be vastly different from one that requires clothes storage within the space. Furniture considerations will change considerably in each, as will task lighting, traffic patterns, and so on. Having a private bath off the bedroom will likewise alter the room's effect, making it seem more stately, important, or private.

Headboards. Elements within the room can also make a big difference. A bulky headboard can be a focal point for a room, while a simple steel frame is more understated. Headboards can be soft (upholstered, padded, tufted, made with elegant fabrics) or hard (wood, plastic laminate, metal, or any other building material), or some combination. The headboard should work well with the proportions of the room while being high enough to lean back on. It's not comfortable, to say the least, to have the headboard reach only the middle of the back when you're digging in with that new novel. Extremely tall headboards are a favorite of mine:

there is something very Hollywood about a tall upholstered headboard that almost touches the ceiling.

Using found objects as headboards is a great way to add unexpected interest and personality to your bedroom. A rusted wrought-iron gate, for example, could be an exciting option in a rustic ranch setting. A pair of old, beautifully paneled doors or folding screens—wooden, latticed, or upholstered—could also work in a variety of settings. I once designed a fencepost headboard, using slats from a picket fence. A headboard can serve a dual purpose: by making it deep enough to house books, you can create a library within your bedroom. When space is tight, a deeper headboard can substitute for nightstands.

Page 100: An upholstered headboard blends with a draped canopy in this lovely bedroom.

Above: The powerful affect of the towering headboard in this room is mediated by its repetitive horizontal lines.

Built-in headboards are useful. I once had clients who had opposing views about clutter: she loved to have everything out and exposed, he was a neatnik. The solution to this potential marriage breaker was to create a built-in headboard that had cabinets with doors on either side of the bed. Behind these doors were small pull-out carts that housed clocks, books, and drawers. Needless to say, her cart was always spilling over, while his was as neat as a pin. During the day, however, the carts simply slid into their cubbies, the doors were closed, and all was peaceful. She still had her clutter, he had his tidiness, and the marriage was saved. The bottom line: let your headboard be a place for personal expression.

Bed Treatments. Beds that are draped offer another great opportunity to make the room special. Few things say romance better than a bed draped in exotic hangings. Historically, bed treatments had more practical than aesthetic value. English and French castles were cold and dark places, where enduring a long winter's night could be a less-than-pleasant experience. Heavy draperies around the bed helped to cut down the cold and drafts, effectively creating a room within a room.

Historically, bed treatments served an aesthetic function as well. In Versailles, the king had an official bed chamber where he met guests; it was a great honor to be invited to the king's bed chamber for his morning rising. He also had a bed chamber in which he slept. Once awakened, he moved to the more decorative chamber to receive his subjects. There's no reason you shouldn't have such a

Left: Two unique headboards show what a focal point this element can be.

Page 103: A draped bed with a full headboard created by "railroading" the fabric, or upholstering it in opposite directions to create a large X. Light reveals the different grains of the fabric, giving the headboard interest and texture.

bed chamber yourself—a little imagination, some exotic fabric, a yard or two of some elegant fringe, and you can have your own regal bedroom.

It's not necessary to go overboard to achieve great effects. Suspending a small, semicircular valance above a bed with side curtains can be beautiful. Line this treatment with a contrasting color or a stripe, or pipe it with a rope trim or fringe, and you have an elegant entryway to your special chamber.

Four-poster beds can be dressed with testers and side panels for a classic look. A more casual approach might involve a single panel draped over poles and suspended a few inches from the ceiling at the head and foot of the bed. Letting this panel fall behind the head of the bed makes a dramatic and stylish statement.

Try everything: old quilts suspended on rods; Grandma's old lace tablecloth; even burlap, canvas, or denim will work. Be as imagina-

tive as possible to make your bedroom truly regal. You may not have another room to sleep in, but you can have an elegant space fit for a king (or queen).

Nightstands. Furniture is another way to make your bedroom special. A nightstand can be both functional and beautiful; it can hold a lamp, give you a place to put a book, and provide a hiding spot for your lotions and creams. Nightstands can also serve as a frame or anchor for the bed, adding personality in subtle—or not so subtle—ways.

Left: Mosquito netting adds charm and whimsy to this inviting daybed.

Above: A tailored, classic look is evoked by the repeated square shape of the headboard, nightstand, and lighting, while the floral arrangement and other accessories add softness and balance.

Page 105: Clutter is hidden behind doors on either side of this built-in headboard. When open, carts pull out for easy access to bedside necessities such as clocks and reading material. When closed, the carts retreat and doors hide everything.

Newsflash: nightstands don't have to match! Asymmetrical bedside treatments can create an interesting bedroom layout. In a recent job, the bed was placed off center within the room because of window placement. This somewhat awkward placement was offset by adding three nested tables on one side of the bed and a conventional nightstand on the other. One of the three tables in the nest was only twelve inches deep but extended four feet under the window, floating behind a lounge chair. The second table, nearly fifteen inches deep by twenty-four inches long, served as a table beside the chair. The third table was about twenty inches deep and only fifteen inches long and became the table for the bed. This unusual arrangement made for a stylish and practical solution in this small but elegant bedroom, and it made the off-centered bed more palatable.

Nightstands can be whimsical as well. When I built my lake house, I spent more than twice the money I had expected to spend. Sound familiar? It happens to us designers as well! I had little money left for furniture. Never let a lack of money limit your creativity! My inexpensive solution: I bought two large galvanized washtubs from the local hardware store. I turned them over and nailed them to two wooden stools I had shortened to the height of the bed, then painted them to match the room. Voila! I had two unusual nightstands for my casual cabin bedroom. If nothing else, these unexpected pieces of furniture caused a lot of conversation.

Creating nightstands to meet your needs is a great way to make your bedroom experience a personal one. Some like drawers to hide all their stuff. Others want open shelves to make it easier to retrieve possessions. Still others just want a simple table to serve as a nightstand. By taking a few minutes to think about your specific needs, you can design a piece that works for you.

Think of your nightstands as jewelry for your bedroom. Just as a special pair of earrings or a beautiful broach can finish that special ensemble, so can properly selected nightstands complete your bedroom. A brightly colored nightstand with an interesting shape and unusual hardware, made from unexpected materials, can make this often overlooked standby a personal and functional addition to your bedroom.

Page 106: Signature pieces, such as a special chair or a large stuffed animal, can be just the element needed to make a room extra special.

Left: This bedroom is designed for people and pets. Notice the special space carved out from under the window seat made especially for the family dog.

Below: Nightstands are not only for books and eyeglasses. Decorate them with flowers and other meaningful objects to create a special setting for relaxation.

Guestrooms

A guest room can be set aside solely as a sleeping room for company or used as a multipurpose room (combined with a home office or den, for example). This room requires special attention in order to maximize its functionality.

One great way to evaluate your needs is to spend the night in your own guest room. Doing so, of course, will help you better know what you need to create the space you'd like your guests to enjoy. It's the little things that make a big difference. A reliable alarm clock, good reading lights, plush towels, comfortable bedding, and special toiletries all work together to create a memorable stay for your guests.

What about the room itself? Is there some special decorative feature that sets the room apart? A beamed ceiling, perhaps, that has an interesting pattern embedded in it? A bay window? Plush comfortable seating with a chenille throw? Any of these features can create a special setting. If you don't have any of these architectural features to set your guest room apart, create them! Here are some ideas:

• Add wooden beams to the ceiling to create interest.

• Add a border molding of several layers of drywall to the ceiling.

• Select a four-poster bed with bed hangings to make a dramatic statement.

• If you have tall ceilings, place the bed on a raised platform for a memorable sleeping experience.

Use your imagination—the more creative your solution, the more unforgettable your guests' experience will be.

Above: Treat your guests like royalty. This four-poster bed with its luxurious fabric treatments ensures a memorable night's stay.

Page 109: Beautiful draperies, luxury linens, decorative wallpaper, and personal mementos make this guest room a welcoming spot.

Bathrooms

Much like kitchens, bathrooms have become more than utilitarian in recent years. In our high-stress world, the bath has become a place of rest and relaxation—a retreat to escape the fast-paced rhythm of our active lifestyles.

A number of years ago, I was asked to create a special bathroom for a design center at a major plumbing manufacturer. They, of course, had certain products they wanted to showcase in the bath. But they also wanted to feature some type of exercise equipment (I'm sure they expected me to put a treadmill or a step-machine in the space). Instead, I added a white canvas punching bag to create an unusual place for relaxation and tension release. We then installed three television monitors and played historical black-and-white footage of historic boxing matches on them.

The point here is to think out of the box. I have seen fabulous baths with indoor gardens, chaises for relaxing, and even built-in saunas. Of course, if you don't have the room, money, or inclination to install a punching bag or sauna in your bathroom, you can still make the space remarkable.

A former colleague remodeled her bathroom by simply installing a low ledge placed about six inches above and along the length of the bathtub. There, she placed a series of votive candles, creating a romantic retreat from the bustle of her everyday life. Another friend removed her tub and created a large shower stall, adding a showerhead at each end of it to create a luxurious spalike space. Something as simple as a heated towel bar can make a big difference. You needn't break the bank to create solutions that are simple, practical, and special.

Page 111: Custom cabinetry and carefully selected fittings dominate this contemporary bathroom, which overlooks a private outdoor garden.

The bathtub itself has evolved recently. The common tubs remain: drop-in units, undermounted tubs, tubs with jets, tubs for two, and soaking tubs, to name a few. But new kinds of tubs are also drawing attention: two of the more intriguing options are vessel and chromatherapy tubs.

Vessel tubs are freestanding, newly styled versions of the old-fashioned claw-footed tubs. Some stand alone with strong contemporary bases, others rest in a wooden support. They're like beautifully crafted sculptures, each creating a unique statement.

Chromatherapy tubs immerse the bather in warm, deep water and, with the touch of a button, flood the tub with a full spectrum of dramatic color. Four LED light ports positioned within the inner walls of the tub allow eight hues to be displayed—emerging, then giving way to the next color. Add to this the sound of water dripping from the rim to the tub's recirculating channel, and you have a rejuvenating bathing experience.

Custom tubs are also popular, often made of unusual building materials. Concrete is an exciting material option; a number of specialized studios can create nearly any shape you can imagine. Just keep in mind that these tubs can be quite heavy and large: make sure that your room will support the weight and that it will fit through your door.

Found objects make great tubs too. At a western ranch, I once used a cattle-watering trough as a tub. (A local rancher's wife who helped me clean it said I was goofy). This unusual tub added character to the special western bathroom.

A watering trough may not be the most appropriate tub for most bathrooms, but neither is a traditional claw-footed model. Take your time and consider all your options—choose the appropriate one to match your personality and the character of your home. Then settle back, light a few candles, and enjoy the experience.

A powder room offers a great chance for a decorator to be creative and experimental — there is no reason why it can't be as fun as it is functional.

Page 112, above: A built-in ledge provides a special place for votive candles transforming the bath into a romantic hideaway.

Page 112, below: A double-sided bathroom provides ample space for two in this beautiful mahogany bathroom.

Above: A bronze basin provides a unique and intimate solution for this naturally clad bathroom.

Page 115: Powder rooms can be as exotic as any in the house. Don't limit yourself to the ordinary!

Powder Rooms

Powder rooms can be extraordinary spaces. Although there are many ways to make powder rooms special, perhaps the most obvious is to play with the plumbing fixtures themselves. Here are some ideas:

Toilets. Toilets come in all manner of shapes, sizes, and colors; some novel varieties can even add a touch of humor to your space. Plumbing manufacturers often reproduce antique fixtures; using an old-fashioned pull-chain toilet might be a fun option for a western or rustic powder room, for example.

Basins. These vessels provide an excellent opportunity to bring a unique look to a space. They sit like bowls on a countertop with a drain hole at the bottom like an ordinary sink. They come in a wide variety of shapes and finishes: clear glass, copper, stoneware, and bronze are just a few of the options available in shapes ranging from semicircular to free-form organic. You can also use found objects as basins: I once used a galvanized bucket as a vessel in a western powder room. The faucets were roughly finished outdoor fixtures, and the bucket sat on a very heavy hand-hewn beam.

Mirrors. Mirrors offer great design opportunities and can make a critical difference in the room. Try different shapes, materials, and textures for your mirror frame.

Lighting. Although you need to provide enough light to see, it is not necessary to flood the space with light. Remember that there are hundreds of options for both fixtures and lamps, so shop around—and don't forget to use dimmers.

The bottom line is that a powder room offers a great chance for a decorator to be creative and experimental—there is no reason why it can't be as fun as it is functional.

Home Offices

Not long ago, the idea of a home office was considered unusual. About twenty years ago, one couple I worked with suggested that we install a computer in the kitchen so they could quickly retrieve their favorite recipes. Everyone thought they were eccentric (a nice way of saying they were crazy), but now their futuristic idea has become commonplace.

A home office can be as simple or as elaborate as necessary. Sometimes these spaces are composed merely of a cabinet or

armoire that has been cleverly designed to house all the necessary office supplies and hardware. It's a great solution for people who have limited space; when closed, this office becomes a stylish piece of furniture that is equally at home in the bedroom, guest room, or even the entry hall.

A home office often requires more than a single piece of specialized furniture, however. For people who earn their living working at home, sharing their space can severely hamper their productivity—home offices that are incorporated into a family room or den are generally not very conducive to serious productivity (or fun, for that matter).

If you're using your home office for occasional work (casual Internet surfing, for example), your options are much more open. Just

Pages 116–117: Whether a dedicated room or a beautiful desk in the bedroom or den, a home-office space has become an almost essential part of any home.

116

- Make certain there are sufficient electrical supplies for all the various hookups. You might consider putting this area of the house on a separate circuit breaker to prevent power outages that can ruin your computer.

- Consider installing a second telephone line, whether for business calls or data (fax or internet). If you're installing high-speed service, be sure you have the hardware you need.

- Consider a lighting solution that reduces glare. Window treatments that cut down natural light might be necessary to ensure that you can see your computer monitor.

- Analyze your work patterns to assure the most functional space. How many books do you need close at hand? Where will you keep your pencils, paper, and the rest of your supplies? Most office supply stores carry supply-management systems; just be sure that the one you choose fits on the tabletop or in the drawers that you have.

remember to make your space both functional and aesthetically pleasing (don't neglect the "home" or "office" aspect of the room). Pay attention to all of the elements of the room, from color and texture to lighting and accessories.

Here are some ideas to make your home office more user-friendly:

- Hide your equipment behind doors. When the doors are closed, the room resembles a paneled library or a sitting room complete with comfortable sofas and chairs. I remember one client who had us add sliding doors to one end of a small television room to hide a home office. Although compact and condensed, the space was very efficient and functional.

Home Libraries

There is something rather magical about a home library. Perhaps it's the idea of curling up in a comfortable chair in front of the fireplace with a good book, or maybe it's the romantic notion of searching for a few words of wisdom in a wood-paneled space with a heavy, rolling library ladder suspended from a brass rail. Regardless of the reasons for its appeal, it's clear that home libraries are making a comeback.

In modern settings, home libraries are often combined with a computer or home-office space. They include comfortable seating and well-designed shelving, becoming at times a secondary living room (albeit one for more solitary pursuits).

If a dedicated space for a library is too much space for you to spare, try combining it with another room in the house. A dining room lined floor to ceiling with bookcases can make a great space; books become accessories for the room, while the dining table can double as a desk. Be sure to run shelving above all the doors and windows, taking advantage of every inch for book storage.

A guest room (or any occasional use room) can double as a library; your guests will never have to search the house for something to read before going to sleep.

When designing these special rooms, spend some time working on the layout of the shelving. Look at your collection of books: do you have a great variety of book shapes and sizes, or are they more or less the same? I'm personally not a fan of adjustable shelving—I prefer to design shelving solutions that are

Pages 118-119: Home libraries offer special places for reading and relaxing. Note how the arrangement of objects on the bookshelves contributes to the atmosphere of each room: a formal feel is created by fewer objects and uniform placement, and a relaxed mood is enhanced by a less structured display.

appropriate for the space and that accommodate the majority of the books. Then, if I must, I provide an additional shelf or two for the oversized and specialty books.

What about arranging the bookcases? Like public speaking, arranging bookcases seems to make people so nervous, they break out in a cold sweat, then never get around to doing it. Relax! There is nothing permanent about your arrangement: you can always change what you've done.

A number of concepts come into play when discussing the art of arranging bookcases. One approach is to mix small pots, objets d'art, and other accessories in and among books; some sit atop books placed on their sides, while others act as bookends. Depending on the objects and the books (and even on the neatness with which it is done), this approach can be formal or informal (though I believe that by its nature it tends toward the latter). As books accumulate and accessories are collected, their placement can become more haphazard; always be mindful of how you add to and take away from your collection.

A more organized and simpler approach to using bookcases is to fill them—as the name suggests—with books. Like the simple black dress, there is something classical and reassuring about the understated presence of a book-only shelf. This doesn't mean that your special figurine, clock, or antique letter box you found at the flea market doesn't have a place on your bookcase—just put it on its own shelf rather than mixing it in with the books. By separating the

elements this way, both your books and your favorite find can be showcased.

Arranging your shelves symmetrically conveys balance. Place bookcases on either side of the fireplace, aligning the shelves. If you put a box on the shelf above the books on one side, put something of similar visual weight on the other side in the same location. Sort the books themselves by size, subject, or frequency of use. If yours is a working library, arrange them in a way that puts the books most often used in the easiest place to reach; if you're just storing your books, keep the heights consistent.

Experiment. Like anything else, the more you do it the easier it becomes. Don't think of arranging your bookcases as a dreaded chore; think about it as an opportunity for expression. Whether you devote an entire room to a home library or prefer to incorporate it into another, remember to relax, have fun, and look forward to the exploring you'll do when you look for new volumes to fill the shelves. Happy reading!

Page 121: This master-bedroom home library features hidden pocket doors that connect the two rooms. The headboard continues the theme and, along with echoing textures and lines of bed and sofa, visually connects the two rooms.

The Wow Factor

Have you ever walked into a room and thought, "There's something special about this place, but I can't quite put my finger on what it is...?" It may not be exceptionally stylish or unique, but it has a certain something—an attitude or presence—that's difficult to describe but impossible to ignore.

This elusive quality—what I like to call the "wow" factor—is what makes a space memorable. It is often achieved with the simplest of elements—a bold color, an overscaled piece of furniture, or even an unusual arrangement of furniture—but it's the difference between an average room and one that makes you stand up (or sit down) and take notice.

I recently visited a friend's beach house. Although this elegant three-story "cottage" was very impressive, one room—a guest room—stood out from the rest. Although many elements made it special, the one I remember most was the way

the walls were painted: large vertical fifteen-to eighteen-inch blue-gray stripes contrasted with a warm pebble color to create a dramatic statement. Not stopping there, my designer friend added a small one-inch high-gloss stripe on top of these larger stripes to further reinforce the dramatic verticality of the room. On either side of the bed was a pair of simple, inexpensive, shaker-inspired oval tables that had been purchased from a local style-conscious department store. These tables were painted the same caramel color of the smaller stripe. The walls and tables worked so well together that I will never forget the room. It was a room with an attitude: a room that inspired a deeply felt "Wow!"

It only takes one or two things to make this kind of impression. Whether it's a painted table, an ornately gilded frame, or a roughly hewn barn table, what matters most is how this single feature says, "This is MY room!"

Above and right: Details like whimsical hand-carved banister posts or a massive, rough-hewn sculpture make powerfully individual statements in these two rooms.

Simplify, then Exaggerate

Early in my career, during an interview with a potential client, I found myself answering a battery of questions I knew the client had recently discovered in a magazine. First he asked me the standard questions—how do you charge and how will we work together? Then, out of the blue, he asked me a question that momentarily stumped me: "What is your philosophy of design?" I had one—or at least I thought I did—but no one had ever asked me to express it. I paused for a second, thought about it, and then blurted out: "Simplify and exaggerate; take an idea to its simplest form, and then blow it out of proportion." I did not get that job, but I have been eternally grateful to that man for helping me to articulate in so few words how I felt about design.

How does this philosophy work? Here are some examples:

• You want to use all brass candlesticks in a setting. Instead of using several types of candlesticks—each in pairs for a total of six to ten for the room—choose one design, and then fill the room with them. Try twenty, thirty, even forty candlesticks.

• Simplify your room's palette to a beige-only color scheme. Then exaggerate by using different patterns, textures, and materials in the room. Try anything beige: furnishings, rugs, accessories, fabric, window treatments—anything.

• Accessorize using books—but don't stop with a few. Cover the room: wall-to-wall, ceiling to floor. No trinkets, no knick-knacks. Just thousands of books.

The key is to try things that seem extreme. Most people are too tentative in their approach to a room. Be bold. Go too far. You can always tone it down later.

Try things that seem extreme. Most people are too tentative in their approach to a room. Be bold. Go too far. You can always tone it down later.

Pages 124–126: Simplify, then exaggerate: various examples of how reducing an idea to its simplest form and then pushing the envelope in its use can be an effective decorating strategy. Whether the simplification involves building materials (p. 125), collections (p. 124 and this page), or palette (opposite), it will provide a stable jumping off point for your experimental exaggerations.

Eclecticism

Chances are you have heard, more than once, someone describe a space as "eclectic." The term has become a catch-all that has almost lost all meaning—when there is no other way to describe or define a certain style, it's eclectic. If you have a room full of furnishings and accessories that seem to have been randomly collected over the years (which may in fact be true!), it's eclectic. But eclectic doesn't mean chaotic—it literally means "choosing what appears best from diverse sources." The key words here are "choosing" and "best"—the principle that distinguishes an effective eclectic room from a disorganized melange of elements is harmony among its elements. Understanding how this harmony is achieved can be elusive—it

requires great sensitivity to style and acute attention to all the elements of design—line, rhythm, scale, proportion, texture, and so forth—to make the room come together. Harmony, when used effectively, it can make a room sing.

Having a common link—however tenuous—among the elements of a room is the most important factor in distinguishing the compelling eclectic room from the wanna-be. When choosing different styles of furniture for the same room, compare them at a variety of levels: consider their texture, scale, line, and so on, but also look at their history and where they came from (a fancy word for this is "provenance"). I once saw the unlikely but effective pairing of a provincial French farm table, rough and worn from years of rural use, with a formal bergère with gilded frames and silk upholstery. Although the two styles were quite different, their common French ancestry and building materials (in this case, wood) unified them. This combination was more effective, say, than if either had been paired with a twentieth-century chrome and leather chair.

**Having a common link—
however tenuous—among
the elements of a room is
the most important factor in
distinguishing the compelling
eclectic room from the
wanna-be.**

In many cases, it only takes one strikingly important and impressive piece that is vastly different from the other pieces in the room to make it an exceptional eclectic room. I am reminded of a wonderful sitting room that I did many years ago. The client wanted a crisp yet comfortable space that incorporated a number of classic pieces of contemporary furniture. What separated this from so many other contemporary spaces was the inclusion of a very large-scaled oil painting the client owned. Housed in an elaborate frame, this classical painting became the anchor of the space. Even though centuries separated these elements, they were still able to work together to create a comfortable and eclectic room.

Top: A common palette keeps an eclectic room from feeling chaotic. Although a variety of decorating styles are used, the underlying stability created by the unifyied color scheme holds this room together.

Accessorizing

A room without great accessories seems unfinished. Without artwork, family photographs, books, or elements on the tables and floor, a space is devoid of interest and character. With accessories, you can make a statement of your individuality, bringing to life a room and making it your own. From choosing plants and lamps to placing found objects, accessorizing is your time to be playful. As with all elements of a room, consider the design principles mentioned earlier in this book (texture, scale, line, etc.) when determining which accessories suit your needs. Have fun and express yourself!

Artwork. One of the best ways to accessorize is with artwork. Many people are daunted by choosing artwork for their walls, then by placing it once they've brought it home. Again, the key is to relax and plan. Here are some tips:

- **Work with the palette of the artwork.** A large and colorful painting can invigorate a quiet, neutral wall setting. A photograph with one dominant color might inspire you to repaint the wall behind it.

- **Consider the scale of the artwork.** A small painting might be lost on a large wall, while another might be too large for its space. The best way to make certain that the scale of your artwork is workable is to draw a scaled drawing of the wall, showing how the painting will look when it is hung. It's easier to move a painting on paper than to drill holes in the wall.

- **Pay particular attention to how your artwork is framed.** The frame's size, material, texture, color, and scale (relative to the painting and the wall on which it's hung) all contribute to making the perfect presentation.

This page: Vases, lamps, books, clocks, plants, and other objects bring the homeowner's personality to the space.

- **Choose appropriate lighting.** Lighting can make or break the presentation of your artwork; after all, if you can't see the painting, it doesn't matter how beautiful it is. The possibilities of lighting are endless and the final solution will depend on the amount of effort you want to expend and the expense you want to incur. If you're remodeling or building, take the time to plan your lighting in advance so that you don't have to settle for a second-best solution. If you're only hanging the painting, consider using picture lamps or track lighting (if you choose this option, be sure to view the artwork from various angles of the room to ensure that the lamp's reflection doesn't block your view of the artwork).

- **Position the artwork to achieve the effect that you want for the room.** The correct height for a picture depends on the picture itself, its setting, the lighting, and its background. "Eye level" is meaningless—whose eye level do you hang to? Are they seated or standing? A better way to judge how high to place the picture is to consider your furniture (is it dominated by horizontal or vertical lines, is it low-lying, or tall?), the sight lines of the room (is a person more likely to sit or stand when viewing it?), and the visual "weight" of the painting (light-colored and smaller images tend to "float," for example, making them appear to be higher than a darker-colored or larger image).

- **Remember the concept of closure.** The spacing between each picture is always critical. Do you want several objects or pieces of artwork to be read as a group? Place them close together. Want to distinguish them? Place them further apart.

Top: Closure is created by framing similar pieces of artwork in similar frames; combined with proper lighting, this picture placement scheme showcases the artwork without overpowering it.

Left: Three black-matted photos attract attention in a home dominated by neutrals. Consider whether you want the art to be bold and striking or quiet and subdued.

Right: The horizontal lines that dominate this interior's decor are enhanced by the panoramic photos and their similarly formatted framework.

- **Avoid the grandmother lineup.** This is an arrangement where photos are hung in stairstep fashion one after another (following the line of a bannister, for example). I once asked my grandmother why she hung pictures that way—she told me she was copying something she had seen on *I Love Lucy*. Don't get me wrong, I am as big a Lucy fan as the next person; she's just not a person I'd turn to for decorating tips.

- **Avoid the studio approach.** In Victorian times, it was the fad to cover a wall with pictures—all sizes, shapes, and frames. I don't think it worked then, and I don't think it works now. An exception might be a family-photo wall, but even then, be sure to employ the concept of closure: use the same or similar frames, and organize the space between the photos so that it suggests unity among them all.

In short, take the time to plan how you want to hang your collection. Draw elevations, look at magazines for inspiration, and, above all, have fun!

Page 132: Large, dramatically colored artwork placed above a mantle creates a focal point that echoes other elements in the room; simplicity, botanical themes, and circular objects are repeated throughout the room.

Top, right: Artwork needn't be framed to be noticed. Here, wall hangings and sculpture take the lead.

Bottom, right: A variety of frame styles and irregular placement make this room interesting and inviting.

Left: Consider alternatives to hanging framed images on the wall. This mantle provides a perfect spot for showcased art. Try them on the floor and on shelves, too.

Natural Objects. Found natural objects make great accents for a room and are inexpensive to acquire—just make sure you're not breaking the law if you're taking them from a protected area! The key to using them is to apply the same principles you've learned for manmade objects—scale, proportion, closure, and so on—so that it's clear they've been intentionally chosen and placed. Here are some ideas for bringing the outside in:

- **Gather a bouquet of branches and tree limbs.** They can be as beautiful as flowers and won't die in a week. Alternatively, fill a large pot with small tree trunks for a similar effect.

- **Stones make excellent decorative elements.** Try stacking river stones on the floor to ground a space both visually and spiritually, or and add a parade of beautifully colored stones to the center of a long table.

- **Tied twigs or dried wildflowers make great hanging elements.** With the wildflowers, you get the added bonus of their wonderful aroma—lavender has a particularly wonderful calming effects.

- **Votive candles work well with many natural elements.** Try wrapping them with leaves or tying them with raffia.

- **Water is an underrated accessory.** Try submerging stones in a shallow container and floating a leaf or blossom above it for an inexpensive and creative arrangement.

- **Sand can bring a contemplative mood to a room.** Create a tabletop Zen garden by filling a flat container with sand raked into a pattern with a fork and highlighted with a choice stone from the garden.

- **Leaves of all colors are beautiful.** Try filling several tall clear glass containers with nothing but the leaves you collect from your favorite tree.

Page 134: Three simple branches and a collection of pinecones unify indoors and outdoors—an inexpensive way to create a memorable centerpiece and bring texture to this contemporary space.

Top: Flowers and plants bring energy and vitality to a room. The simple flower arrangement here works with the scale of the other display objects to create a balanced, informal setting.

Above: A collection of branches from your own backyard can add textural variety to a room. Notice how triangular lamps and the diagonal lines of the branches add interest to a space dominated by vertical and horizontal lines.

Above: Simple elegance is created by highlighting a few select accessories at a time. Rotate pieces occasionally to refresh and revitalize a space; an accessory closet can help store your other favorite objects to avoid cluttered displays.

Page 137: Arranging accessory pieces into groups or pairs is a way to showcase many items while avoiding visual clutter.

Accessory Closets. When you are out shopping, do you ever see a special object and think how nice it would look on the bookcase in the living room, only to remember that the bookcase is already full of accessories? In fact, not only is the bookcase full, but so is the table, the sideboard, and the rest of the house. What's an accessoryholic to do?

The answer is to create an accessory closet—a place where you can put some or most of your favorite accessories out of sight to be rotated back into the room on a regular basis. You needn't have everything you love on display at the same time—by moving, changing, and rotating these treasures, you make each piece special. And just think how exciting it will be to refresh your room with your favorite object every month!

Here are some tips for setting up your accessory closet:

• If you have no closet space, try taking those old clothes, golf clubs, and broken holiday decorations to the local thrift shop! You'll feel better twice: once when you clean out the clutter, and again when you display your favorite decorations with the dignity they deserve.

• Try using the guest coat closet. When was the last time you put coats in there? Chances are that most of those coats go on the bed. Why not take that space, or at least half of it, for your accessories?

• If you are lucky enough to be building a house, make sure you plan a special accessory closet. You'll be thankful later.

• Lay out your closet wisely. Plan for a lot of varying adjustable shelves so that objects can be retrieved without stacking or storing them several deep or high.

• Don't put your accessories in boxes! Out of sight is truly out of mind: if you can't see your objects, you'll probably forget them and not rotate them as often as you might like.

• If possible, make some shelves only six to eight inches deep. Consider a kitchen-type storage unit that allows for only one layer of objects. Tray or drawer–style storage will help you rotate small paintings and photographs.

• Create special spaces for lamps and shades. If you really do not have room for these larger accessories, try moving them from room to room.

The point is to use your accessories like paint on a palette. Remember that accessories make the room your own: even if you don't have a lot of money to spend, take the time to put the right finishing touches on your room. You'll be glad you did.

A Final Word

You now possess the basic tools to get started on your home! You've learned the ABCs of decorating, you have the vocabulary to communicate and learn more about what we've covered, and now you have developed the greatest tool in design: awareness. A ceiling has become a new opportunity for creative expression. Floors and walls have become blank canvases. Rooms have become more than just individual elements within your house. You have new accessory options and an approach to implementing them, and you've seen examples of how to make the ordinary extraordinary. What's next? That's up to you. Start now to create that dream space—that special bedroom; that warm, inviting living room; the kitchen that is the envy of chefs everywhere. With the basic guidelines we've covered, you're well on your way to making your spaces come alive with function and personality. Enjoy!

Designers

Alternative Design
New York City, New York
Pages 40, 99, 112

Atlanta Homes & Lifestyle
Page 69

Beth Beaudoin Interior Design
Atlanta, GA
Pages 32, 72, 91, 104

Brito & Chalgub, Inc.
Miami, FL
Pages 42, 63, 76, 99

C. Kantola Interiors, Inc.
Pages 94, 107, 112

Century Architectural Specialties
Marietta, GA
Page 52

Charles Gandy, Inc.
Atlanta, GA
Pages 6, 17, 26, 74, 75, 113, 142, 144

Colour Corps Interior Design
Nashville, TN
Page 60

Edwin J. Rabine & Company
Atlanta, GA
Pages 85, 108

Epperson Design, Inc.
Atlanta, GA
Pages 7, 24, 73, 102

Epperson/Gandy (Brad Epperson & C. Gandy)
Atlanta, GA
Pages 5, 7, 12, 13, 18, 26, 39, 49, 63, 126, 135

Essary & Murphy, Inc.
Atlanta, GA
Pages 14, 20, 24, 27, 28, 29, 35, 36, 38, 47,
48, 54, 58, 64, 70, 77, 78, 81, 82, 84, 87, 89,
90, 92, 100, 106, 109, 118, 119, 125, 126,
133

G. S. Hinsen & Company
Nashville, TN
Pages 19, 23, 90, 96, 137

Gandy/Peace (Charles Gandy & Bill Peace)
Atlanta, GA
Cover, Pages 3, 6, 7, 11, 14, 16, 17, 19, 26,
33, 36, 37, 38, 53, 55, 56, 57, 59, 79, 86, 93,
101, 103, 105, 106, 111, 114, 115, 117, 121,
127, 129, 130, 132, 134, 136, 138

Guyton Design Group
Atlanta, GA
Pages 15, 34, 44, 46, 50, 51, 135

Home Magazine
Pages 45, 61, 88, 98, 124, 126

Jerry Pair
Atlanta, GA
Pages 54, 84, 85, 90, 97

Joy McLean
Page 97

Joye Hirsch Interior Design
Atlanta, GA
Pages 2, 32, 70

Marshall Howard Interior Design
Atlanta, GA
Pages 24, 107

Mary Gannon Stencils
Pages 22, 43

Miner Details
Atlanta, GA
Pages 45, 67, 71, 122

Nancy Pickard Interiors
Montgomery, AL
Pages 30, 35

Patti Krongold Design
Atlanta, GA
Page 123

Peace Design
Atlanta, GA
Pages 20, 73

Pineapple House Interior Design
Atlanta, GA
Pages 41, 91, 131, 138, 139

Portland Cement
Page 110

The Authors

Romantic Homes
Page 98

Southern Accents
Pages 66, 96

Stanley Ellis, Inc.
Atlanta, GA
Pages 25, 36, 74, 95, 110, 116

Susan K. Goans
Atlanta, GA
Pages 40, 41, 52, 83

Suzanne McCallen Interior Design
Franklin, TN
Pages 21, 95, 133

The Iron Gate
Franklin, TN
Pages 9, 28, 31, 104, 128

Todd Bienz, Inc.
Atlanta, GA
Pages 32, 72, 91, 104

Todd White
Atlanta, GA
Page 73

Veranda
Pages 59, 74, 95, 110, 116

Westbrook Interiors, Inc.
Atlanta, GA
Pages 65, 76, 80, 90, 102

Charles D. Gandy, FASID, has designed interiors across North America for more than three decades. Former National President of the American Society of Interior Designers, Mr. Gandy is the coauthor of Contemporary Classics: Furniture of the Masters. As a nationally recognized designer, he has lectured to thousands on design. His column, Design 101 (where much of the material here first appeared) runs weekly in the Atlanta Journal-Constitution.

Chris Little, a photographer based in Atlanta, Georgia, specializes in corporate and residential interiors and advertising photography. He has photographed for many award-winning designers, shot Fortune 500 annual reports, and traveled the globe on numerous international projects. His photographs appear in many national magazines as well as design-related books.

Acknowledgments

Special thanks go to all the clients and designers whose work appears on these pages. To my many colleagues who helped me create such special spaces, especially to Bill Peace, my former business partner, and to Chris Little, for his keen professional eye. Thanks, too, to many mentors and friends: Steve Ackerman, Hugh Latta, Brad Epperson and Bill Willard, Donna and Doug Burbank, Karen and Gil Hardwick, Steve Demand, Judy Barber, Jerry Pair, Richard Maxwell, Carolyn and Larry Howard, and, of course, the Neely Family.

Charles D. Gandy

I count my blessings each and every day for the talents God has given me and for my devoted wife and loving children.

Much appreciation and thanks to the wonderful and gifted clients I have had the privilege to work with over the years. You continue to inspire me wth your imaginative design and creativity.

A special note of thanks to my friend, career-long client, and author of this book, Charles Gandy, whose design expertise made this book possible.

Chris Little

Special thanks to Dixie Little for her skills in editing, to Joseph Little for his technical creativity, and to Johnny Caine for his many talents as photo assistant.

Index

Accessorizinng 129-137
    artwork, choosing and
    dispaying 129-133
    natural objects 135-137

balance 28-31
    symmetrical 28-30
    asymmetrical 31

basins

bathrooms 110-113
    bathtubs 112

bedrooms 101-107
    headboards 101
    bed treatments 102
    nightstands 104-107

ceilings 50-52

closure 36-39

color 60-63
    color schemes 62-63
    monochromatic color 62-63
    analogous color 62
    complementary color 62

dining rooms 92-97
    dining room chairs 95-97

doors 52-54

draperies 55

eclecticism 126-128

embellishments 64-85

entry halls 88-89

fabric 76-79
    warp and weft 79
    denure 79
    hand 79
    aesthetics 79

floors 45-48
    concrete 45-46
    bamboo 46
    terrazzo 46
    cork 46
    wood 46
    exotic wood 46

focal point 90, 91, 102

form 26
    cubes 26
    cylinders 26
    spheres 26
    cones 26

furniture 70-75
    arrangement 73

guest rooms 108-109

home libraries 118-121
    bookcases, arranging 120

home offices 116-117

lighting 56-59
    general lighting 56
    acccent lighting 58
    task lighting 58

line 12, 16-19
    horizontal 16
    vertical 17
    diagonal 19
    curved 19

living rooms 90-91

kitchens 101, 102

mass 32-33

mirrors 88, 96

mood 26, 32

nightstands 107, 110, 112, 114

paint 50-52, 60

pattern 35

powder rooms 114
    basins 114
    lighting 114
    mirrors 114
    toilets 114

proportion 40-41

rhythm 20, 23
    regular rhythm 20
    irregular rhythm 20
    progressive rhythm 23

scale 23-25

shape 26

texture 34

variety 40-41

walls 48-50

windows 55

window treatments 80-84
    soft and hard 80
    draperies 80
    valanced 83
    cornices 83
    hardware 84